Discover Gin

Chin, chin....here's to gin! And here is the book to help guide you through the extremely pleasant task of discovering gin.

It is a tasting course that takes a close look at the many facets of the world of gin, its roller-coaster history, how it is made, why it is the basis of so many cocktails, and how we are witnessing a fantastic resurgence in this drink.

There is also a guide to the top distilleries in the UK and the tremendous number of artisan, hand-crafted distilleries that have emerged all over the country.

The book looks at the history of these gin makers and hears from some fascinating characters...from the UK's Mr Gin, who has a lifetime of experience, to exciting newcomers to the gin-making business.

They all agree that the wonder of gin is that there appears to be no end to the very different ingredients that can be used in its making...juniper, coriander and citrus fruits, of course, and then there are even more lip-smacking elements such as liquorice, rhubarb, seaweed, and even frankincense and myrrh.

As the distillers become more adventurous in their search for greater varieties of gin so has the popularity of gin soared. Small hand-crafted distilleries continue to blossom and bars devoted to enjoying gin have opened all over the country.

So this is the perfect time for a leisurely leaf through the pages of *Discover Gin* as you find out why so many of us throughout the world are saying cheers! to gin.

John Millar

Picture: Alistair Devine.

Publisher
Ken Laird

Lang Syne Publishers Ltd.
79 Main Street,
Newtongrange,
Midlothian
EH22 4NA
Tel: 0131 344 0414
E Fax: 0845 075 6085
E-mail: info@lang-syne.co.uk
www.langsyneshop.co.uk

Written by **John Millar**
Special Advisor **Edwin Atkinson**
Design **Dorothy Meikle**
Print **Warners Midlands plc**

Gin Gen

- Some 70 percent of gins produced in the UK are made in Scotland.

- Like the Queen Mother before her, The Queen enjoys a gin and dubonnet. Prince Philip's gin tipple is a Silver Bullet – a gin cocktail that incorporates Kummel, lemon juice and sugar syrup.

- In 1269, juniper-based tonics were listed in a Dutch publication.

- The French claim they have been involved in gin making for over 450 years.

- Genever is made with malt wine – a mixture of malted barley, wheat, corn, and rye – which produces a fuller-bodied spirit. A small number of genevers in Holland and Belgium are distilled directly from fermented juniper berries.

- In Germany there is a Genever style Gin called Dornkaat. It is found in the North Sea coast region of Frisia. This spirit is lighter in body and more delicate than Genever and Dry Gin. German Gin is usually served straight up and cold.

- There are more than 700 gin cocktail recipes.

- Dutch gin may be jonge, which is youn, or oude, which means aged or mature.

- The Dakota, Cheyenne, and Pawnee tribes had juniper on their wigwams to keep their homes safe from storms.

- The Plymouth distillery that is owned by Pernod Ricard was founded as Coates & Co in Plymouth and claims to be England's oldest working gin distillery. It is next door to the refectory where the Pilgrim Fathers spent their last night before sailing to the New World.

- In 1777 Edinburgh had eight licensed distilleries and an estimated 400 unlicensed.

- Navy Strength gin goes back to the days when gin and gunpowder were stored alongside each other on board a vessel. Navy Strength gin is 57% abv because if the gin was accidentally spilled on a ship's gunpowder then this strength of alcohol meant that, even if soaked, the gunpowder would still light.

- The juniper berry in Britain in an endangered species. Most distilleries source juniper from Tuscany, Bulgaria and Egypt. The berries cannot be cultivated or mechanically harvested and are picked by hand.

- After juniper, coriander is the second most commonly used botanical in gin.

- During the making of gin, the distiller will MACERATE the juniper berries. Macerate means softening or separating into parts by steeping in a liquid.

- ABV is the abbreviation for alcohol by volume. This is a standard measure of how much alcohol is contained in a given volume of an alcoholic drink. The ABV standard is used worldwide. ■

Gin & Ten

What is Gin?

Gin is a rather dry alcohol which is flavoured with the berries of the juniper bush.

How did Gin get its name?

It's reckoned that the name comes from the Dutch word 'genever' which means juniper. There is also a theory that it comes from the Swiss city of Geneva.

What are the main types of Gin?

There are four main types of gin...London Dry Gin, Dutch Genever, Old Tom and Compound Gin. London Dry Gin is the most widely available and, despite its name, does not have to be produced in London. The name is defined by the manner in which the gin is made. London Dry Gin is made by redistilling grain alcohol with botanicals and adding nothing after the process of re-distillation. Dutch Genever has a process more like whisky. It starts with a malted grain mash and utilises barrel-ageing. Old Tom uses sugar in re-distillation and is a sweeter gin. Compound Gin uses essences that are added to the grain spirit and there is no re-distillation. Hendrick's is a type of compound gin: the signature cucumber and rose petal essences are too delicate for the re-distillation process and are added after the other more traditional botanicals are re-distilled with neutral spirits.

What is Plymouth Gin?

Only one brand exists today of the gin, which is not as dry as London Dry Gin. It's called Plymouth and is produced by the Black Friars Distillery, the only remaining gin distillery in Plymouth. It is now owned by Pernod Ricard. Plymouth Gin is a Protected Geographical Indication. Which means it is a gin that is made within a specific region and possesses unique properties.

What are the botanicals used in making Gin?

A fine gin is reckoned to contain six to 10 'botanicals'. These are natural elements that include juniper, nutmeg, coriander, citrus peel, cardamom, cinnamon, almond or liquorice that can be used to flavour the grain alcohol.

Why was the invention of the continuous still significant?

Also known as the Column Still, this invention made the process of making a pure base spirit much more cost effective and allowed the uses of more subtle flavours and botanics. The device is also known as the Coffey Still, after Irishman Aeneas Coffey who received a patent for this two column still in 1830. After its creation the use of the new still was taken up worldwide.

Has Gin really been credited with having medicinal qualities?

Yes. Mid-way through the 13th Century there was talk of the use of tonics that were juniper based. Of course the Navy famously used gin mixed with lime to try and prevent scurvy. In the tropics gin and tonic (because of the quinine in the soft drink) was seen as a method of avoiding malaria.

Is Gin the Cocktail King?

There is certainly an excellent argument for it to be given that title since there are more classic cocktails made with gin than with any other spirit.

What is the strength of Gin?

In the European Union the minimum bottled alcoholic strength for gin is 37.5% ABV. Whereas in the USA the minimum strength of gin is 40% ABV. (Alcohol by volume).

What is Sloe Gin?

Sloe gin is made with gin and the fleshy fruit of the sloe berry. The sloes are soaked in gin during a procedure that lasts for at least three months at the end of which time the liqueur is poured off and the leftover sloes can be thrown away or used for jam or chutney. ∎

Beefeater

20 Montford Place,
London SE11 5DE.

If James Burrough had used the formal name of the colourful character with whom he'll be forever associated, there wouldn't have been enough room on the bottle label of the gin that he first produced way back in 1863.

For the official description of the ceremonial guardians of the Tower Of London that Burrough featured as the company's very distinctive logo is The Yeomen Warders of Her Majesty's Royal Palace and Fortress the Tower of London, and Members of the Sovereign's Body Guard of the Yeoman Guard Extraordinary.

Rather a mouthful. So it's just as well that the Devon-born founder of the company went for the more popular and far simpler title, Beefeater.

Now Beefeater is based in London's Kennington, a hefty six away from the legendary Oval Cricket Ground.

Originally though, in 1862, Burrough set up shop in Chelsea when for £400 he bought from James Taylor the distillery which stood in Cale Street, between King's Road and Fulham Road.

Among the gins produced by Burrough were James Burrough London Dry, Old Tom, Ye Old Chelsea and, of course, Beefeater.

The recipe for Beefeater to this day remains a secret that is known only by the Master Distiller.

The original Beefeater recipe book of 1895, listed nine botanicals...juniper, angelica root, angelica seeds, coriander seeds, liquorice, almonds, orris root, seville oranges and lemon peel...but of course it is the proportions that are so vital to creating the finely balanced gin.

The company remained in Chelsea till 1908 when larger premises were sought and the move was made to Lambeth.

This new distillery was named Cale Distillery, thus retaining the link with its origins.

Fifty years later, in 1958, production moved again; this time to Kennington and John Dore, the famous manufacturer of English stills, was asked to build a bigger set of copper stills.

When the layout of the distillery was designed by Norman Burrough, in collaboration with the architects, Douglas and J.D. Wood, it meant that for the first time the bonded warehouse and bottling hall were brought together with the still house, under one roof.

At that time the offices and the duty paid cellars remained at Beefeater House in Vauxhall Street.

Tasting Notes

BEEFEATER LONDON DRY
"Classic London gin aromas. The clean citrus aroma of Seville orange peel develops into more complex notes from juniper and coriander. On the pallet, citrus again leads through to the classic piney flavour of juniper in the middle taste. The finish is a long and gentle journey through spicy coriander and angelica to a sweeter finish from almond. Beautifully balanced and complex throughout."

BEEFEATER 24
"The subtle note of green tea at the start hints of more complex aromas to follow. A hint of grapefruit opens up to the classic aroma of juniper and spice. The flavour begins with gentle notes of spicy citrus that form on the pallet to deliver the classic juniper taste that is supported by the softer tannins from the selected green teas used in Beefeater 24. The long finish demonstrates the benefit of the unique process of steeping all the botanicals in pure spirit for 24 hours before distillation."

BEEFEATER BURROUGH'S RESERVE
"Taking the original Beefeater recipe and then rested in rare Jean de Lillet oak barrels, Beefeater Burrough's Reserve was created to be savoured neat, with different temperatures and glassware subtlety changing the aromas and flavours of this unique spirit. On the nose, floral spice and vanilla notes develop into soft juniper aromas. The palate shows soft and complex spice. Subtle citrus flavours lead to a distinctive juniper middle-taste, returning to a gentle spice on the finish."

Master Distiller Desmond Payne.

The floors of the still house section of the building were removed and replaced up to third floor level by specially strengthened concrete floors.

This third floor and the second floor accommodate the new stills, with a 38 foot headspace to the new roof for the tops of the rectifying columns. The third floor level houses the control platform.

Two oil fired boilers are required to provide for the steam, central heating and hot water. With a rating of 10,000 pounds of steam per hour each, they provide an ample reserve for all requirements.

On the roof there is a reservoir for storing water with a capacity of storing 30,000 gallons drawn from the firm's own well below the distillery.

On the floor below the stills there is a battery of Prodor-Glas lined reception vats for the finished gin and the various blending operations.

The bottling hall, which is in the bonded warehouse, contained three bottling lines, two fully automatic, with an output of 300 dozen bottles an hour each, and the other semi-automatic, with an output of 75 dozen an hour.

The gin is pumped from the still house to a weigh tank of 4,000 gallons capacity, mounted on a 20 ton scale, then weighed and the "drawback" of duty assessed by Customs and Excise before passing to storage tanks in the bottling hall.

Machines dry and automatically discharge the bottles for delivery to all-stainless steel filling machines fed from the storage tanks.

After filling, the bottles are capped automatically. At this stage one of the few manual operations follows...the "sighting", or scrutinising of each bottle to detect any possible imperfection.

Then they are fed to labelling machines and afterwards wrapped in Cellophane.

To effect a smooth co-ordination of the bottling and packing operations, empty fibreboard cases are brought to the bottling hall by conveyor.

After packing, the cases are fed to a gluing and taping machine and then left on conveyors to the storage bays above. Each case is counted automatically as it passes a photo-electric cell system.

The Burrough family sold out to Whitbread in 1987 and in 2005 the company was acquired by the Pernod Ricard group.

Today Beefeater proudly boasts that all of its 2.4 million

BEEFEATER'S BOTANICALS

Although the amount of each botanical that is used in the recipe for Beefeater remains a closely guarded secret, Beefeater admit that this recipe has changed little since the days of James Burrough. Beefeater's crisp, clean, well balanced flavour is derived from 100% natural ingredients, known as the botanicals, which are brought to the London Distillery from all over the world.

The principal botanicals in Beefeater Gin are juniper, coriander and the citrus peels that provide freshness and lift. The other botanicals in the recipe add complexity and depth.

The best juniper grows wild on mountain slopes in Italy and Macedonia. Crops vary from year to year so, every September, the Master Distiller samples the harvest to create the exact blend of berries he requires.

In Beefeater Gin the distinctive oily, piney taste of juniper is the palette on which is layered the subtle flavours of all the other botanicals in the recipe.

Coriander seeds are the second most important botanical in gin. The most highly flavoured coriander comes from Romania, Russia and Bulgaria.

When distilled with the other botanicals, coriander seeds release ginger, sage and lemon flavours.

These combine perfectly with the strong citrus elements of Beefeater Gin to produce a spiciness and freshness that linger in the mouth.

Coriander also contributes to Beefeater's dry peppery finish.

The crisp, sharp flavours of Spanish lemons add another dimension to Beefeater's strong citrus profile.

Only the peels are used and they are dried in the sun to enhance their rich oiliness.

Original recipe books at the Distillery, in James Burrough's hand demonstrate his use of orange peel as a major botanical in his gin recipe.

Ever since then, Beefeater Gin has had a more citrus character than other gins.

Seville oranges, commonly found in marmalade, impart the fresh, clean, citrus notes that make Beefeater Gin instantly recognisable.

Bitter almonds, ground to release their oil, are also an essential part of the Beefeater botanicals profile.

Almond brings a hint of marzipan and nuttiness while at the same time adding to the complexity.

The earthiness of angelica root, from Flanders in Belgium, is what makes Dry Gin dry.

Its woody, spicy notes also contribute to creating a complex yet integrated botanicals profile where, clustered around the distinctive keynote of juniper, no single aromatic overpowers.

Long ago the art of distilling was closely related to that of alchemy. As with alchemical processes, balance and harmony are all important when making gin.

Angelica seeds impart fragrant, hop-like notes with a floral character, a counterpoint to the muskiness of angelica root.

The liquorice comes from China. It contains natural sugars, bitter compounds, and a substance that produces the characteristic woody, bittersweet flavour, all of which are crucial to the underlying spiciness and mellowness.

Liquorice also softens and rounds out gin's mouth feel.

Ground orris root, from Italy, is an essential part of the botanicals mix.

Aromatic and floral in itself with a hint of Parma Violet, orris also holds the volatile elements of the other botanicals together and allows their subtle flavours to slowly and gently build.

Juniper.

Coriander.

Oranges.

Liquorice.

Orris Root.

9 litre cases each year are made in the Kennington distillery, which has undergone a massive face-lift.

There is now a conference facility that holds up to 150 people. The visitor centre, opened in 2013, serves as a mini-museum, complete with a replica of James Burrough, there is a new bar that was added in 2006 and the reception, boardroom and botanicals room have also been renovated.

The history of gin is a vital part of the experience offered by the Beefeater visitor centre.

Starting in the 18th century with Hogarth's infamous 'Gin Lane' drawing, key milestones in London's gin history are brought to life through an interactive experience which takes visitors through the cobbled Victorian street markets of Covent Garden to the secret watering holes of the Prohibition era.

Fans of the spirit will learn more about the fragrant botanicals used in the creation of gin during the tour, which continues with a walk through the production process in the distillery's cathedral-like still house and ends with a complimentary drink – the classic Beefeater gin and tonic.

Another innovation is the Beefeater Gin School – which was originally a large bonded whisky warehouse – capable of holding up to 500 guests.

The Gin School extends over the course of two days, when guests may visit the Beefeater distillery, learn how Beefeater gin is produced and receive cocktail training.

Telephone: +44 (0) 20 7587 0034
Email: info@beefeaterdistillery.com

Blackdown Sussex Dry Gin

**Blackdown Artisan Spirits,
Lurgashall, West Sussex GU28 9HA.**

The setting for the first gin to be produced in Sussex just has to be described as poetic. After all the distillery is amid sprawling woodland near where Alfred Lord Tennyson, the writer of such epic works as *The Charge Of The Light Brigade,* once lived.

And the Dry Gin that was launched by Sarah and Nathan Thompson in the summer of 2013 pays homage to the local land.

Because the special ingredient in their gin comes from the trees through which it is conceivable that Tennyson might have strode.

The couple add to the more traditional botanicals something that you might say gives their gin bark and bite!

It is sap from the silver birch trees that populate their 40 acres or so and which is drawn from the trees each Spring.

But the silver birch isn't invited to the party until right at the end of the process.

First juniper, angelica, cassia bark, orris root, liquorice, cinnamon, bitter orange zest, sweet orange zest, lemon zest, coriander and nutmeg is blended with pure water and charcoal filtered seven times before the silver birch sap is added after distillation.

Since the distillery is surrounded by a forest of silver birch it might appear that it was always a given that the woodland would play a part in Sarah and Nathan's gin making.

But Sarah admits that it happened by accident. She had an idea that the silver birch would work to compliment the other botanicals and knew that it was an ingredient that can be used in wine making.

So she decided to experiment and came up with a gin that confirmed that she was justified in following her intuitions.

Although they are in the infancy of their small batch gin making – producing around 7,000 bottles a year of their handcrafted product – the couple have long been a part of the drinks industry.

Apart from gin they also produce vodka, vermouth, black cherry liqueur and elderberry port.

The couple plan to also start developing some other varieties of gin.

**Telephone: +44 (0) 1428 748204
Email: enquiries@blackdowncellar.co.uk**

A Bird Cherry Martini.

Tasting Notes

*APPEARANCE:
A clear, bright liquid.*

NOSE: A delicate gin, with traditional woody aromas; the predominant notes are Juniper, Coriander, Citrus and Silver Birch.

TASTE: Full of flavour and slightly sweet with a very smooth and refined mouth feel.

FINISH: Traditional citrus finish, smooth and refined on the palate.

Bombay Sapphire

Laverstoke Mill, London Road,
Whitchurch RG28 7NR.

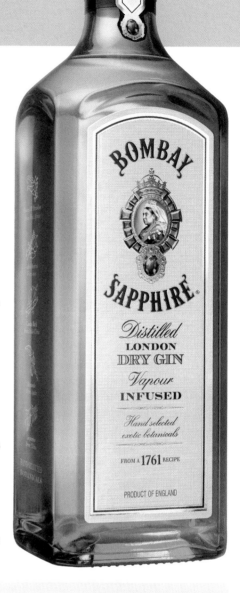

Early in 1761 earthquakes, that caused structural damage, were recorded in London. But other ground shaking news that year came when legendary English distiller Thomas Dakin created a very special gin recipe.

It's on that historic recipe that Bombay Sapphire was based when it was launched in 1987.

The name Bombay Sapphire comes from the popularity of gin in India at the time of the British Raj. The sapphire is the 182 carat sapphire which was named, The Star Of Bombay. It was bequeathed to the Smithsonian Institution by the Hollywood film star Mary Pickford, who was given the jewel by her husband, Douglas Fairbanks.

Now it is sold worldwide, across 120 markets, and significantly, Bombay Sapphire retains its historical link with Thomas Dakin.

Bombay Sapphire was the first premium gin to showcase the importance of botanicals, which are hand-selected from exotic locations.

There are 10 botanicals – selected with care by Ivano Tonutti, Master of Botanicals.

These are...juniper berries from Italy, Spanish almonds, lemon peel that also comes from Spain, Chinese liquorice, orris root from Italy, angelica from Saxony, Moroccan coriander, Indo-Chinese cassia bark, cubeb berries from Java and grains of paradise that are sourced from West Africa.

A global collection of goodies!

And the final touch to the award-winning gin, that in 2008 was hailed as the fastest growing major international premium gin, is that it is encased in a unique and striking translucent blue glass bottle that bears the iconic image of Queen Victoria.

The latest innovation from Bombay Sapphire, which is now owned by Bacardi, has been to move from Warrington to be based at the stunning, brave new world of Laverstoke Mill, where the chalk stream waters of the River Test runs through the centre of the new distillery.

As with its origins, Bombay Sapphire has with its new home again been immersed deep in history.

There has been a Mill on the Laverstoke site since the 10th Century and Laverstoke Mill is listed as a corn mill in the Domesday Book of 1086.

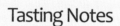

Tasting Notes

"Nose: Pine green juniper, coriander, lemon, floral notes with spice, underlying woody notes. Palate: Lemon zest with medium sweetness, balanced with complex spice at base of palate. Finish: Sweet dry balance, integrated lemon spice character, underlying light woody notes."

The Botanical Dry Room, showcasing the 10 botanicals used to create the unique flavour of Bombay Sapphire.

The historical Dakin Stills used in the unique Vapour Infusion process at Laverstoke Mill.

The botanical glasshouses, designed by Thomas Heatherwick and Heatherwick Studios, taking centre stage at Laverstoke Mill.

More than 600 years later, in 1719, it became a paper mill when a French Huguenot called Henry Portal converted it to make the finest quality hand-made paper, for the bank notes of the British Empire.

Naturally it was a delicate and patient task to transform such an ancient and historical structure into the Bombay Sapphire distillery, especially since it is a Conservation Area and a site of Special Scientific Interest.

The centrepiece of this striking modern building is inspired by Britain's rich heritage of Victorian glasshouse structures.

It is the two intertwining Botanical Glasshouses – one tropical, one temperate – specifically designed to showcase examples of the 10 hand-selected botanicals from around the world, used in every bottle of Bombay Sapphire gin.

Laverstoke Mill also features the Empire Room, a training centre where masterclasses will be hosted for trade and media guests from all over the world.

In October 2014 the distillery was opened to the public and tours are available during which you can be plunged into the exotic world of Bombay Sapphire.

It's a different distillery experience that involves a taste of ancient history, a walk along the River Test, a tour of the Glasshouses where the botanicals are stored and a behind the scenes visit to the Vapour Infusion distillation process in the Dakin Still House.

Telephone: +44 (0) 1256 890090
Email: hello@bombaysapphire.com

Bombay Sapphire Distillery at Laverstoke Mill.

Picture: Iwan Baan.

Booth's

Felix Booth.

Though it is no longer made, Booth's Gin has a rich and fascinating history, stretching back to the earlier part of the 18th century.

The company produced two London Dry style gins – Booth's Finest and Booth's High and Dry.

To promote them Booth's published *An Anthology of Cocktails* in the 1930s, which featured cocktail choices and photographs of society figures and well-known characters of the period, such as Ivor Novello and Lady Oxford.

Booth's were pioneer exporters of gin and have played a leading role in establishing the global reputation of distilled London Dry Gin.

In 1850 Booth's was granted the right to bottle British spirits in bond for export and, as a result of this, Booth's became an international brand.

Up until the 1940s Booth's Finest was the UK's number 1 gin.

Before World War II, Booth's Finest Dry Gin was matured in Sherry casks for three years.

Advancements in distillation techniques then rendered the cask ageing part of the process unnecessary, but Finest Dry still retained its unique "wood mellowed" characteristics.

Since it has been discontinued, Booth's Gin is sought after by gin collectors. But if you are chasing down a bottle you need deep pockets because it can cost well in excess of £100.

Red Lion Distillery.

BOOTH'S TIME LINE

1740 Booth's is founded in Clerkenwell.

1780 It is said that Philip Booth armed his workers with muskets and prevented the distillery from being pillaged during the Gordon Riots, which began as an anti-Catholic protest in London. Numerous other distilleries and breweries were sacked by the mob. Now the muskets are held at the Diageo Archive.

1829 The Duke of Clarence, later William IV, visits the Brentford Distillery. Felix Booth finances (at a cost of £20,000) the second expedition by Captain John Ross to discover the elusive North-West Passage. As a result, Booth's is permanently associated geographically with Canada: a large section of the Dominion's Arctic north is named the Boothia Peninsula. There is also Cape Felix and Felix Harbour.

1831 Felix Booth elected Master of Coopers.

1840 Brentford Distillery is distilling a million gallons a year. Felix adds a Scottish branch of the company and a cognac distillery. He starts the manufacture and supply of coal gas and founds the Brentford Gas Company.

1941 A German incendiary bomb is extinguished in a 200 year old still in the Turnmill Street Distillery.

1986 Distilling at Clerkenwell ceases.

The Distillery in the 1960s.

A selection of Booth's adverts from throughout the 1930s.

Boxer Gin

Greenbox Drinks Ltd, 1A Hazlewood Tower, Golborne Gardens, London W10 5DT.

Since the idea was a gin that packed a bit of a punch, it followed that the most obvious name would be Boxer Gin. This interest in the ancient art of pugilism produced ideas for the artwork on the back of the bottle.

Hours of research at the British Library and poring over archives of the *Sports Illustrated News* magazine played a part in all of that.

Ultimately the distillers decided on reworked antique engravings of real characters from the history of boxing. The fighter who is featured on the back of the bottle is English 19th Century Heavyweight Champion Tom King.

Nicknamed 'The Fighting Sailor', King was arguably the first undisputed Heavyweight Champion of the world after his defeat of American Champion John C. Heenan in 1862.

When he retired as the undefeated World Champion he then made a fortune as a successful bookmaker and married an heiress.

Deciding on that king of the ring for their label came after company managing director Mark D. Hill had experimented on distilling their first gin.

Using an antique copper teapot that he'd bought in London's Portobello Road, and a home-made condensing unit, Mark worked away in his kitchen.

Reflecting now on that process, he says that the very first batch was actually very good.

After that he was off and running. Or perhaps that ought to be punching!

Using Angela, a still that was hand-made in Bethnal Green over 100 years ago – Boxer Gin was born.

Mark believes that the copper used to make the still was reclaimed from the hulls of scrapped British naval warships.

Since he is a Londoner born in maritime Greenwich there would seem to be a nice symmetry to the origins of Boxer Gin.

Significantly, Mark stresses that Boxer Gin uses fresh juniper berries and he claims they are the only company currently in production that uses fresh rather than dried berries.

The botanicals in Boxer Gin are common juniper, juniper indica, coriander, bergamot, sweet Seville orange, sweet lemon, angelica root, orris root, liquorice root, cinnamon, cassia bark and nutmeg.

The first step in the preparation of Boxer Gin is the distillation of a soft, pure wheat spirit; using the highest quality grain from the east of England.

Tasting Notes

"The main balance of flavours is between fresh juniper and the triumvirate of citrus – lemon, orange and bergamot. This extra dry balance is set against a background of rich, woody spice and aromatic floral roots. The Boxer difference is most apparent on the nose and on the finish, it stands up exceptionally well to tonic, remaining clear even on heavy dilution."

The botanicals in Boxer Gin are common juniper, juniper indica, coriander, bergamot, sweet Seville orange, sweet lemon, angelica root, orris root, liquorice root, cinnamon, cassia bark and nutmeg.

This grain is fermented and distilled using a combination of a modern tower still and a veteran copper pot still.

The result is a gentle, soft spirit with a natural grain sweetness and subtle flavours of grass and hay.

The next step is to distil a classic London Dry Gin.

They steep the botanicals in the copper distilled wheat spirit, to allow the flavours to be released into it.

After an eight hour maceration, the mix goes into the 108 year old copper pot still – which is gently heated until the spirit is turned into vapour and then condensed back into a liquid. This process fixes the botanical flavours into Boxer gin.

In order to deliver an added vibrancy to Boxer Gin they have created a new process in the production.

They separately steam distil fresh, wild juniper berries to extract their essential oil.

This 20 hour process is carried out at source in the Himalayas.

Similarly, they also extract a zingy raw citrus essential oil by cold pressing fresh bergamot peel.

The final stage is the marriage of wild juniper and organic bergamot essential oils with the gin; and the addition of pure, sweet Sussex spring water to open up the flavours.

In addition to Boxer Gin, which they export to 12 countries, the company makes Bloodshot Spiced Vodka and Element 29 Vodka.

Telephone: +44 (0) 20 7183 0711
Email: info@gbdrinks.com

Broker's London Dry

Shepperton, Surrey TW17 8AG.

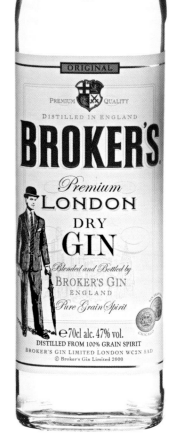

To celebrate the very English flavour of their Gin, Broker's use a distinctive Bowler hat theme. Which is why every bottle is topped by a miniature Bowler! And Martin and Andy Dawson, the brothers who founded the company wear Bowlers as a promotional gimmick.

The company name Broker's comes from the notion that Bowlers would be worn by City of London stockbrokers.

Broker's Gin was created initially with the focus on export. Apart from the UK, the company now sells in all 50 US states, all major provinces in Canada, and about 50 other countries around the world.

The distillery where Broker's Gin is made is located near Birmingham and is over 200 years old.

There had previously been a brewery on the site, but this was converted to a distillery at a time when gin-making became more profitable than beer-making.

The distillery uses only traditional pot stills. Continuous distillation using column stills is more efficient and is used by the major brands, but pot stills extract maximum flavour from the botanicals in a traditional hand-crafted fashion.

The distillery has a mini-still, which is used for making small batches of gin from different recipes. The recipe for Broker's Gin is 200 years old and was chosen after taste-testing against several newer recipes.

The copper pot still used for producing Broker's Gin is named "Constance" and was manufactured by John Dore & Co, long recognised as the finest still-maker in the world.

The base spirit for Broker's Gin is quadruple-distilled pure grain spirit made from English wheat. The flavour is provided by 10 natural botanicals, the primary one of which is juniper berries – as in all gins.

The botanicals are steeped – soaked – in the base spirit in the still for 24 hours. This is the first part of the flavour-infusion process. The still is then fired up for the final, fifth distillation, which completes the process.

The distillery where Broker's Gin is made is located near Birmingham, England and is over 200 years old.

Tasting Notes

"Clear, rich, creamy, candied citrus and fruit peel aromas. Very smooth on the palate with a good balance of fresh botanicals, spicy juniper and sweet, ripe citrus fruit. Finishes with a smooth, warming, peppery fade. A delicious and stylish gin with the guts to stand up to tonic as well."

Andy Dawson and the distillery's mini-still, which is used for making small batches of gin from different recipes.

comes out of the still first and what comes out of the still last, are set aside.

After the distillation process has been completed, the used botanicals are discarded.

Even after distillation, individual botanicals can be identified. The round, purple berries are juniper. The small round, brown seeds are coriander. The large yellow lumps are lemon and orange peel. The stick-like pieces are cassia bark or cinnamon bark. The other botanicals are powders, which are dispersed throughout the mix.

Telephone: +44 (0) 1932 22 88 00
Email: broker@brokersgin.com

Trevor Fletcher places juniper berries into the still.

Botanicals are sourced from all over the world and shipped to the distillery in sacks. The botanicals used in Broker's Gin and their sources are...Juniper berries from Macedonia, Bulgarian Coriander seed, Cinnamon bark from the Seychelles, Indonesian Cassia bark, Orris root from Italy, Polish Angelica root, Nutmeg from India, Italian Liquorice, Lemon peel and Orange peel from Spain.

The botanicals are added to the still in carefully measured quantities according to the recipe. Some botanicals, e.g. juniper, require a number of sack loads.

Where quantities smaller than a sack load are required, a small shovel is used.

During the distillation the Master Distiller assesses the quality of the spirit at the spirit safe. Only the "heart of the run" is retained. The "heads" and the "tails", in other words, what

A perfect Martini should
be made by filling
a glass with gin, then
waving it in the
general direction of Italy.
– *Noel Coward, writer, actor*

I'll stick with gin.
Champagne is just ginger ale
that knows somebody.
– *Hawkeye, US TV series, M.A.S.H*

Gin by pailfuls, wine in rivers.
Dash the window-glass to shivers.
– *Sir Walter Scott,*
novelist, playwright, poet,
Guy Mannering

Burleighs

The Collection Yard, Bawdon Lodge Farm,
Nanpanton Road, Leicestershire LE12 9YE.

Inspiration can come at you right out of the blue. When you least expect it or while you are in the process of something seemingly quite mundane.

As renowned master distiller Jamie Baxter discovered that lightning bolt of inspiration can even strike to make the ordinary become extraordinary.

Baxter was enjoying a stroll through Burleigh Wood – a woodland reserve near Loughborough – when he was confronted by some of the wonders of nature.

He came across an array of silver birch, dandelion, burdock, elderberry and iris and was so thrilled by this discovery of seeing these botanicals in the one place that they went on to inspire the original recipe for what became Burleighs London Dry Gin.

They became five of the eleven botanicals that are used to create the smooth, crisp and complex flavours of the gin.

And it was, of course, a no-brainer that the ancient Leicestershire woodland area of natural beauty should give the gin it's name.

The gin is handcrafted at the 45 West Distillery which is located at a farm that is in the Charnwood Forest which is next to Burleigh Wood.

Burleighs Gin is made in Messy Bessy, which is the name given to the handsome copper pot still.

Visitors are welcome to 45 West Distillery which is home to a Gin School where the art of distilling gin may be discovered under the tutelage of master distiller Jamie Baxter.

The visitors can, of course, have the pleasure of bottling and taking home their own gin.

There are three varieties of Burleighs Gin – Signature, Export Strength and Distiller's Cut.

Export Strength and Distiller's Cut , with an ABV of 47 per cent, are slightly stronger than Signature.

In addition to their trio of gins, the company also produces Urban Vodka, Kiska Vodka, Absinthe and liqueurs.

Telephone: +44 (0) 116 278 8492   Email: sales@45w.co.uk

Tasting Notes

SIGNATURE
NOSE: crisp and fresh with piney eucalyptus and fragrant citrus to the fore.

PALATE: big, robust flavours with an initial hint of dry juniper followed by pine, eucalyptus and citrus. Spicy and floral notes in the background.

FINISH: long with Parma violet, pine and eucalyptus with warming, dry peppery notes.

EXPORT STRENGTH
NOSE: Crisp and fresh with piney eucalyptus and fragant citrus.

PALATE: An initial hint of dry juniper followed by pine, eucalyptus and citrus and spicy and rooty notes in the background.

FINISH: Long with Parma violet and eucalyptus with warming, dry peppery notes.

DISTILLER'S CUT
NOSE: Crisp and fresh with piney eucalyptus and fragrant citrus.

PALATE: An initial hit of juniper with floral, earthy, spicy dry notes followed by citrus.

FINISH: Long with Parma violet, pine and eucalyptus with warming, dry peppery notes.

The Burleighs Botanicals

Caorunn

Balmenach Distillery, Cromdale, Strathspey PH 26 3PF.

Pronounced 'Ka-roon', Caorunn is the Gaelic word for rowan and is a small batch, hand crafted gin. It is produced in the Balmenach Distillery whose history of whisky making dates back to 1824.

Caorunn is the first gin to be produced at a working malt whisky distillery in the Scottish Highlands.

The award-winning gin's inspiration comes from Celtic tradition, which is why the special botanicals include hand-picked ingredients that grow wild and in profusion in the Speyside countryside that surrounds the distillery.

These local crops are rowan berries, of course, Coul Blush apples (which are the most northerly grown apples in the UK), heather, bog myrtle and dandelion.

The other six botanicals in the recipe are the more classical ones for gin...juniper, coriander, lemon peel, orange peel, angelica root and cassia bark.

Caorunn comes in a

Balmenach Distillery.

Tasting Notes

"On the nose it's juniper with fruity notes of rowan and apple that develops beautifully into clean, crisp, aromatic flavours with a pronounced fruitiness and slight heather honey sweetness. A long dry finish makes this one for those who are fans of versatile, mellow gins."

Caorunn Botanicals spread evenly on 4 perforated trays of the Copper Berry Chamber.

called Copper Berry Chamber, made in the 1920's.

The chamber is round and contains four large perforated trays on which the botanicals are placed.

As the vapour passes through the trays of the Copper Berry Chamber it picks up the flavours of the botanicals in a long slow process.

When it cools and returns to liquid, now 96.6 % gin, the flavours and aromas of the botanicals are firmly embedded in the spirit.

The spirit is distilled four times and it is during the fourth distillation that the botanicals are infused.

The makers recommend that a Caorunn G and T should be served with a thin wedge of red apple...preferably the Pink Lady variety.

Caorunn was launched to the UK market in August 2009. During the course of the past five years it has won more than 25 awards globally for its versatile taste and distinctive packaging.

It is considered as one of the most successful craft gin brands in the UK. (Nielsen, IWSR).

Apart from the UK Caorunn is now available in 25 countries, including Canada, New Zealand, Mexico, Singapore, Malaysia, Spain, the USA and Australia.

striking five-sided bottle which represents the five locally foraged sourced botanicals.

Caorunn is made using a variety of unique botanicals, its flavour profile is slightly different from classic London style gins, it is less juniper heavy. Caorunn is a Modern London Dry Gin with its aromatic, fruity, floral notes.

A unique vapour infusion method is used for Caorunn, so an exceptionally pure neutral grain spirit is heated to vapour before it reaches the special still

Telephone: +44 (0) 870 888 1314
Email: contact@caorunngin.com

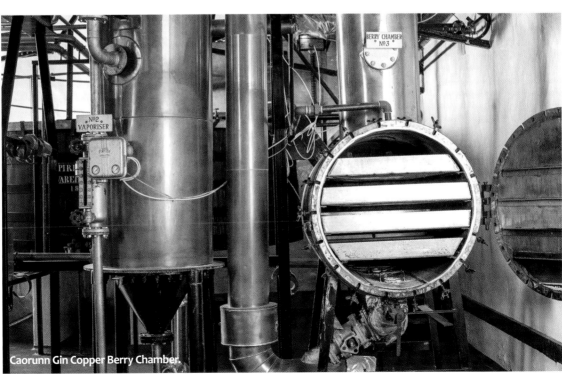

Caorunn Gin Copper Berry Chamber.

Copper House

Adnams plc, Sole Bay Brewery, Southwold, Suffolk IP18 6JW.

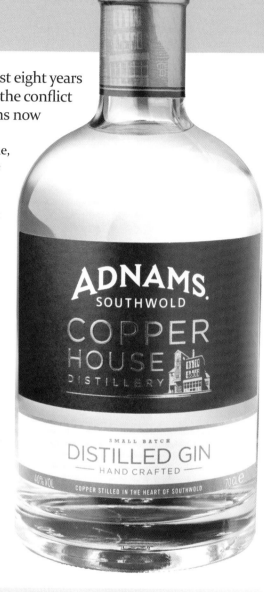

The Hundred Years War between England and France was just eight years old and a new war weapon – cannon – was introduced into the conflict when beer was first brewed at the Suffolk site where Adnams now have their brewery and distillery.

It was 1345, the year when England were victorious at the Battle of Auberoche, when back on the other side of the Channel, Johanna de Corby and 17 other 'ale wives' of Southwold were charged by the manorial court with breaking the assize of ale.

From those beginnings Adnams has gone on to have a colourful history as it built towards a successful and eventful future.

The Adnams brothers, George and Ernest, purchased the Sole Bay Brewery in 1872. But George clearly had his eyes on wider horizons than the Suffolk countryside.

He left Southwold for South Africa and it was out there that he was reportedly 'eventually eaten by a crocodile'.

By 1890 Adnams & Company was established and went on to achieve an enviable reputation as beer brewers.

More than a century later, in 2008, Adnams opened its energy efficient brewery and produced the UK's first Carbon Neutral beer.

Significant steps into the production of spirits began in 2009 when the distillery project – the Adnams Copper House Distillery – was started and the first distillation took place in October 2010.

Just four months after producing Adnams Copper House Spirits, they began winning awards at international competitions.

Where Adnams had a natural advantage as a brewer was that they were able to produce their own base vodka-quality alcohol – used to make gin – through their beer brewing process whereas many other gin manufacturers buy in industrially-produced neutral grain spirit to produce gin on a mass scale.

Utilising the brewing process ahead of distilling gin also enhances the natural and distinct flavours which make Adnams gin unique.

Copper House gin is distilled from East Anglian malted barley where a beer

Copper House Distillery.

Tasting Notes

"Copper House Gin – an easy drinking fruity floral gin which works well in a Gin & Tonic. This gin shines through with its big juniper and fruitiness from the hibiscus."

"First Rate Gin has a more complex profile with a great balance between the botanicals. Used in a G&T you will pick up different botanical mix with each sip. A gin of choice for the classic martini."

The stunning view across the rooftops to the Lighthouse.

'wash' is made which is fermented to around 6% ABV without the addition of hops before being run through a beer stripping column which removes all the alcohols to create a 'low wine' of 80-85% ABV.

The 'low wines' are distilled in a hand-made copper pot still and purified further before being returned to the copper pot still to be redistilled and infused with six botanicals to impart their delicate aromas and flavours before they are diluted to 40% or 48% ABV and bottled.

The distillery sits in the room which used to house the old brewing coppers. From the top of the building are stunning views across the rooftops to the Lighthouse and North Sea.

The Gins that Adnams produces are...

Copper House Gin which has the following botanicals – juniper berries, orris root, cardamom pods, coriander seed, orange peel, hibiscus flowers.

First Rate Gin which uses these botanicals – juniper berries, orris root, cardamom pods, coriander seed, orange peel, lemon peel, fennel seed, caraway seed, angelica root, cassia bark, liquorice root, thyme and vanilla pods.

In 2012 Adnams for the second time, won the Queen's Award for Enterprise: Sustainable Development.

Telephone: +44 (0) 1502 727200
Email: info@adnams.co.uk

When a man who is drinking
neat gin starts talking
about his mother
he is past all argument.
– C.S. Forester, novelist,
The African Queen

I would like to observe the
vermouth from across the room
while I drink my Martini.
– Winston Churchill,
former Prime Minister

Of all the gin joints in all
the towns in all the world,
she walks into mine.
– Rick Blaine;
Played by Humphrey Bogart
in the film Casablanca

Cotswolds Distillery

Stourton, Shipston-On-Stour CV36 5HT.

Set in five acres of Cotswolds countryside, this distillery – which opened in the summer of 2014 – boasts of being 'the most beautiful distillery in England.' During the build, their Scottish distillation equipment was transported more than 500 miles from the Forsyth's plant in Rothes, Speyside and is well underway in the creation of the first Cotswolds single malt whisky. The first batch Cotswolds Single Malt is distilled from local organic Cotswolds barley and will be ready for limited release in 2017 after the minimum three year ageing period.

The Distillery is also in production of its Cotswolds Dry Gin; a traditional London dry style with the addition of a Cotswolds twist! Locally sourced raw materials are at the heart of this new gin, including Cotswolds Lavender sourced only 10 miles from the distillery.

Cotswolds Dry Gin has a blend of nine carefully-considered botanicals. The expression of the traditional London dry style comes from the maceration into pure wheat spirit of juniper, coriander and angelica root, which have been left overnight to allow their flavour characteristics to fully infuse.

To this is then added a unique botanical mix of Cotswolds lavender and bay leaf, fresh grapefruit peel, fresh lime peel, black pepper and cardamom seed into their Holstein still for distillation before finishing with naturally refined Cotswolds water.

A bonus for gin lovers is the decision by Cotswolds Distillery to create a Single Botanical Distillate Library on site. Alex Davies, Head Distiller at the Cotswolds Distillery, and his team have overseen the distillation of a 151 strong (and growing) single-botanical distillate library, the first of its kind on this scale.

This library explains exactly how each botanical behaves under distillation, and ultimately how its flavour characteristics will come across when distilled. The aim of The Cotswolds Distillery is to use this flavour profiling in helping with recipe development and as an educational tool, explaining the nature of distilling and helping visitors to identify individual botanicals within a gin recipe.

The distillery will also produce a number of more contemporary style gins and other spirits, including an English Rye Whisky and Cotswolds Cider Brandy. Distillation will result in incredibly small-batch spirits to be released as limited editions from 2015 onwards.

Telephone: +44 (0) 1608 238 533   Email: info@cotswoldsdistillery.com

Cotswolds Distillery.

Tasting Notes

"Nose: fresh citrus notes of grapefruit upfront with a hint of earthy coriander backed-up harmoniously by sweet floral notes of juniper. Upon deeper inhalation, soft notes of cracked black pepper become apparent with a hint of minerality and perfumed Cotswolds lavender.

Palate: clean, pine spice from the juniper comes through on entry, closely followed by fresh grapefruit and a hint of coriander seed. A little black pepper spice builds with a touch of dryness from the angelica root before light mineral and eucalyptus notes appear from the bay leaf. The lime works its way in right at the end before the subtle lavender shows itself.

Finish: Clean and balanced. Juniper, citrus and some cooling notes from the bay leaf and cardamom."

Dà Mhìle

Glynhynod Farm, Llandysul, Ceredigion SA44 5JY.

Welshman's Caviar is how the legendary film star Richard Burton described laverbread, a traditional Welsh delicacy. It is of course a dish made from an edible seaweed that is found along the Welsh coastline.

Laver is created by first boiling and then pureeing or mincing the result to make laverbread, which can be eaten with bacon or cockles or to accompany lamb or seafood.

This variety of seaweed is such a part of the Principality's culinary experience that it is not really a surprise to discover that the local seaweed would be used in the creation of a very Welsh gin.

Dà Mhìle Seaweed Gin was crafted as a drink to compliment seafood and is one of the latest spirits

Seaweed and light.

Tasting Notes

SEAWEED GIN Nose: "As soon as I opened the bottle, I got a massive, herby whiff that was green and inviting, but also very warm. I poured a measure, took a sniff, and was blown away by the heady mixture of vibrant herbs and spices. There's an aniseedy fennel type scent, a pepperiness, delicate lemon thyme, and a gorgeous nose-filling cardamom aroma that really sealed the deal. Maybe it's all in my head, but I felt the seaweed also added a mineral, seasidey element."

Taste: "This all follows through on the palate, with the addition of a slightly bitter orange, and the hint of something fruitier. It's certainly less sweet than the luscious, gingery Warner Edwards, and warming in a different, spicier way, and lacks the juniper in-your-face-ness (some might say overkill) you can get with better known brands."

Overall: "If you're looking for a new, exciting gin to try, this is SO IT. And it's the kind of gin you'll always want a bottle of in the cupboard to brighten a dull day. Impressively, the distillery sells it in 50ml, 350ml and 700ml bottles, so you can even buy a wee one to experiment – but I warn you, it's likely you'll be re-ordering pretty quickly."

- Laura Vickers, Vinspire UK

The Tasting Gallery.

created by the distillery launched by John Savage-Onstwedder, one of the founders of the renowned Teifi Farmhouse Cheese.

Savage-Onstwedder is an organic farmer who commissioned the Springbank Distillery in Campbeltown, Scotland near the Mull of Kintyre to produce the world's first organic whisky of the modern era.

That whisky was made to commemorate the millennium and is why the Welsh distillery was named Dà Mhìle, which is pronounced 'da-vee-lay' and means 'two thousand' in Gaelic.

That whisky is highly rated and is now the oldest barrelled Springbank in existence. A second batch was commissioned from Loch Lomond in 2000.

Gin was added to the repertoire as the company was expanding the cheese business on their farm in west Wales.

A dedicated dairy building was established, meaning that the old dairy was without use. John Savage-Onstwedder explored the options of installing a distillery.

With part government funding and the inevitable tussles with building regulations, in 2010 the first product made was an Orange liqueur – called Orange 33 – which won a true taste award for its first batch. A year later it won a prestigious GREAT TASTE Award.

Soon after, gin production started. The idea was to create a full bodied, heavily botanical gin.

The first few batched contained 20 botanicals, although this has slowly been refined to 18 over the years.

As mentioned seaweed is a very traditionally Welsh dish that is widely used in Welsh cooking.

The company even makes a seaweed cheese.

It's Seaweed Gin, which has a distinctive green colour, was launched on March 1 – St. Davids Day – in 2014.

"With some subtle tweaks to the botanical recipe we managed to completely change the gin base," explains Dà Mhìle distiller, Mike Melrose.

"Even without the seaweed infusion it has a very subtle hint of the seaside, fresh and crisp with a slight salinity in the finish.

"How did we achieve this? By adding 'unusual' herbs and spices…things you'd usually use while cooking fish or scallops – Marjoram, Parsley and Thyme are a few without giving too much away."

This seaweed gin is made with a cut-down, hand selected variant of botanicals to Dà Mhìle's small batch gin and is infused with fresh seaweed from the Newquay coast for three weeks, before being triple filtered and bottled.

"The infusion with the seaweed gives the gin its light green hue and solidifies the salinity, giving it more prominence through the duration," says Melrose.

"In summary, we created a fantastic aperitif to seafood dishes, and at the same time we made the ultimate base to any 'dirty' cocktail…an intriguing and obscure green gin with a naturally salty baseline."

(A dirty martini contains a splash of olive brine or olive juice and is typically garnished with an olive. A perfect martini uses equal amounts of sweet and dry vermouth.)

Distiller Mike Melrose stresses that the future of the distillery is paramount on producing top quality.

"It may take us time to release new products but we want people to know they're receiving the best, because the pursuit of excellence is written into our DNA," adds Melrose.

"We have a few things in the pipeline, including a Whey Vodka, Apple Brandy and Absinthe."

Dà Mhìle encourage visitors to the distillery.

There are tours round the distillery, showing all parts of the process and there is a tasting gallery.

There are plans for an optics bar and it is intended that the work of local artists will be displayed.

Telephone: +44 (0) 1239 851528
www.damhile.co.uk

The Distillery.

Darnley's View

Wemyss Vintage Malts Ltd,
4 Melville Crescent, Edinburgh EH3 7JA.

JE PENSE

The beginning of one of Scottish history's most tempestuous romances – it ended in the violent death of the husband – was the inspiration behind the name of this Scottish boutique gin.

Darnley's View marks the moment, on 17th February 1565, when Mary, Queen of Scots spied on the man who was to become her second husband, Henry Stuart – Lord Darnley.

The story goes that Mary secretly watched from a courtyard window when Darnley visited Wemyss Castle...which is pronounced 'Weems'.

She obviously liked what she saw because after meeting formally the couple fell in love and were married that July at the Palace of Holyrood.

So when the Wemyss family decided to add gin to their drinks portfolio – apart from producing hand crafted malt whiskies, they have a long standing connection with distilling going back to the 19th century when John Haig built his first distillery on Wemyss land – their thoughts turned towards the legendary royal connection with Wemyss Castle.

And in 2010 they launched Darnley's View London Dry Elderflower And Citrus Gin, a classic gin with balanced juniper and citrus, and a surprising twist in the form of fruity and floral elderflower.

Two years on they brought out Darnley's View London Dry Spiced Gin, based on a recipe that the family worked on with gin expert Geraldine Coates.

Keeping up the strong family image of the product, the gins feature a swan which is the Wemyss family logo.

Darnley's View is distilled five times in the London Dry style according to a family recipe using six botanicals...juniper, coriander seeds, lemon peel, angelica root, orris root and elderflower.

Ten botanicals are used for Darnley's View Spiced Gin...juniper, cinnamon, nutmeg, cassia, grains of paradise, ginger, cumin, cloves, coriander seed and angelica root.

The botanicals are macerated in neutral grain spirit for 15-24 hours before distillation and then the distillation takes four hours in batches of 300 litres.

Wemyss Castle.

Tasting Notes

DARNLEY'S VIEW *"Nose: Clean, fresh and vibrant with the aromas of juniper being very distinctive. Palate: Juniper coming through strongly, sharp citrus and mellow spice with laid back floral notes.*

Finish: Long and dry, with a twist of floral and fruit characters from the elderflower."

DARNLEY'S VIEW SPICED GIN *"Nose: Big spice, with almost toffee aromas to the fore. Palate: Full and rounded, cinnamon and nutmeg coming through strongly, with juniper developing gently."*

DARNLEY'S VIEW COCKTAILS

THE LORD DARNLEY

Ingredients:
50 ml Darnley's View
dash Bottlegreen Elderflower cordial
dash Fevertree Tonic Water
dash Limoncello
dash Angostura Bitters

Method:
In a mixing glass filled with cubed ice, add the Elderflower, Tonic, Limoncello and Bitters coating the ice. Stir and drain off any excess liquid. Add the Gin and still well chilled and suitably diluted. Double strain into glass straight up.

Glass: Champagne Saucer

Garnish: Maraschino Cherry

MARY QUEEN OF SCOTS

Ingredients:
50ml Darnley's Spiced Gin
75ml tomato juice
12.5ml freshly squeezed orange juice
Juice half lime
3 dashes Tabasco (to taste)
2 teaspoons Worcestershire Sauce
2 grinds cracked black pepper
2 teaspoons fino sherry
celery salt

Method:
Run a lime wedge around the rim of the glass and then dip the wet rim into the celery salt. Fill the glass with cubed ice then pour in Darnley's Spiced Gin, tomato, lime and orange juices and the Tabasco and Worcestershire sauces. Float sherry on top and grind black pepper over top too.

Glass: Hi Ball

Garnish: Celery Stick

SPICED EAST INDIA DAISY

Ingredients:
Gin
50ml Knops IPA
12.5ml freshly squeezed lemon juice
12.5ml freshly squeezed orange juice
12.5ml grenadine (home - made)
Soda

Method:
Pour all ingredients (except IPA) into a shaker over cubed ice and shake rapidly. Single strain into glass over crushed ice. Charge with IPA.

Glass: Pewter Mug

Garnish: Stem of red currants, bramble, orange wedge

This is blended with neutral grain spirit and then reduced to bottling strength with de-mineralised water.

The neutral grain spirit is currently wheat based and sourced from Manchester and the fifth distillation takes place at Thames Distillery in south London.

The results have been multiple award winning gins that are sold world-wide...in the UK, France, Germany, Holland, Belgium, Austria, Switzerland the USA and nine other countries.

Telephone: +44 (0) 131 226 3445
Email: info@darnleysview.com

Edinburgh Gin

1A Rutland Place, Edinburgh EH1 2AE.

Picture: Alistair Devine.

Alex and Jane Nicol set out from the start to be the creators of a capital gin. Now they are the only 'Edinburgh Gin' since 'Edinburgh Gin' is their trade mark which they registered five years ago.

Gin was produced in Edinburgh until 1974 when the last distillery closed and Alex and Jane wanted to restore that tradition.

The parent company, Spencerfield Spirit Company, was started on 25 July 2005 after Alex Nicol who had been steeped in the drinks industry for many years – his last position was CO of Whyte And Mackay – decided to do his own thing and bought the Sheep Dip and Pig's Nose whisky brands from Whyte And Mackay. But what the couple always wanted to do was produce gin.

They did some experimental work before bringing out the first Edinburgh gin in 2009. It was very juniper forward. A typical London gin – since nothing is added after distillation, except water – but they wanted to give it a Scottish twist. Hence Edinburgh Gin was born.

To do this pine, milk thistle and heather was added. The result was pleasing and the next step was to buy stills and find the optimum place in Edinburgh in which to be based.

Getting the right venue, which turned to be an atmospheric and spacious cellar in Rutland Place, took two years.

Getting the copper stills, which when full weigh three tons, down into the cellar was an issue. Walls had to be knocked down and it took the best part of a day to lower the stills into position.

Alex and Jane Nicol.

Tasting Notes

Edinburgh Gin *"Very floral aroma, giving a lot of heather and quite citrusy with a sharp orange and lemon after taste."*

Cannonball Gin *"Gives a very big juniper hit on the aroma with quite a bit of spice and the initial flavour has a massive amount of juniper which then gives way to a long spicy after taste of the Szechuan pepper."*

Christmas Gin *"A sweet but slightly spicy aroma and then you get a tongue coating mouth feel followed by a warm spicy after taste from the nutmeg."*

coriander, orange, lemon, angelica, orris, liquorice, cloves and cassia. Then of course the Scottish elements...pine, milk thistle and heather.

Their supplies of juniper are hand-picked on the Bulgaria-Romania border.

The next gin to be created was Cannonball Gin, which of course creates a link with the legendary cannon, Mons Meg, at Edinburgh Castle.

This is a stronger, Navy strength gin which has an added kick that is provided by Szechuan peppers that are used instead of more delicate botanicals such as heather and pine.

And in the winter of 2014 another, very special gin was added to their repertoire...a Christmas Gin which has an infusion of frankincense and myrrh!

Getting the ingredients, of course, means more globe trotting. The myrrh comes from Somalia and the frankincense from the Middle East.

Frankincense provides a dry after taste and perfumy notes in the aroma whilst the myrrh has a thicker mouth feel and is very sweet and so off-sets the frankincense.

They also do gin fruit liqueurs, with flavours such as rhubarb and ginger. Scottish botanics are used, such as raspberries from Blairgowrie, local elderflowers, and rhubarb from Inverness.

They have been commissioned to produce a spiced gin for customers in the Far East.

Among future plans is producing a 200th anniversary gin for Scottish Widows.

Telephone: +44 (0) 131 656 2810
Email: info@edinburghgindistillery.com

In 2013 the distillery reckoned to have produced around 60,000 bottles of gin. That mark had been passed by the time they were midway through the following year's trade.

Expansion is in the Edinburgh Gin mind-set. They have calculated that they are capable of producing more than 200,000 bottles per year and they intend to have another still set up in a second location in another year or so.

Edinburgh Gin already have international distribution, supplying France, Holland and the USA.

In order to protect their title, the company applied for and got the European trademark for Edinburgh Gin.

To create Edinburgh Gin, they researched old Edinburgh gins and modified these recipes to come up with their own product...which is a traditional gin made with wheat grain spirit which the makers believe is cleaner and lighter.

The classic botanicals are used...juniper,

David Wilkinson, Head Distiller at the Edinburgh Gin Distillery.

David has been working at the distillery since June last year. He graduated from Heriot-Watt University with an MSc in Brewing & Distilling in 2013 and is currently on a graduate scheme known as a Knowledge Transfer Partnership. This is a collaboration between Heriot-Watt and Spencerfield Spirits where he is employed by the university but carries out the majority of his work on site at the Edinburgh Gin Distillery.

He is in charge of new product development and the commercial production of gin recipes for the company, this is complimented by research work into botanicals carried out at the university. Here David is operating one of the miniature (2 litre) stills. These are used for product development as they can make several very small batches using different botanicals in order to design gin recipes. When a recipe has been finalised it is then scaled up and produced on the commercial (150 litre) stills then is bottled by hand on site and either sold in the distillery shop or sent to suppliers.

G&J Distillers

Melbury Park, Clayton Road,
Warrington, Cheshire WA3 6PH.

H istory and resilience combine to form the remarkable story of this Warrington-based outfit which defied the trauma of a disastrous blaze to rise from the ashes.

Today the business is part of the international drinks group, Quintessential Brands, which took it over in 2011.

That is the latest manifestation of the leading distiller and bottler of spirits in the country.

G&J have been in business for more than 250 years, making it one of the oldest gin distilleries in the world.

It all started in 1761 when the legendary Thomas Dakin formed Dakin's Warrington Gin.

Then, towards the latter half of the 19th century, Edward Greenall bought over the company from the Dakin family and it became G&J Greenall....named after Edward's younger brothers, Gilbert and John

So began a dynasty that carried the proud motto "I strive higher", and lasted several generations, till 2006 when the final family connection ended when Lord Daresbury left the company.

It goes without saying that the history of this company – which apart from its own gins, distills and bottles other labels, such as Bulldog and historically Bombay Sapphire and also produces vodka – is very impressive.

The longevity is even more astounding when you consider that across those three centuries the company has only had seven Master Distillers!

Which is where the resilience comes in. Because just a few years ago – in 2005 – the very existence of G&J was threatened by a horrendous fire that gutted the building.

The warehouse was utterly destroyed but the stills were saved

Tasting Notes

"With a rich herbaceous and citrus aroma, Berkeley Square has notes of juniper, basil and sweet lime which lead to a long peppery finish. The first taste of Berkeley Square Gin confirms the quality of the ingredients and the careful, slow distillation that goes into creating this 'single malt' of gins."

Greenall's Wild Berry Gin's inspiration came from blackberries growing in English hedgerows, combined with raspberries which are infused in award-winning Greenall's Gin to

Picture: © Jason Lock Photography.

give a vibrant, fruity taste.

Tasting Notes: "Luscious & juicy berry notes balanced with juniper and warming spice. The smooth mouth feel lasts, leading to peppery after tones."

Greenall's Sloe Gin is made with hand-picked sloe berries, slowly macerated in Greenall's The Original London Dry Gin, for a rich, deep naturally flavoured sloe gin.

Tasting Notes: "Rich and fruity, with gentle juniper and spicy flavours, this smooth

Botanicals being put into the still.

and the plucky outfit were hardly knocked off their stride; and within a week they had restarted distilling.

A move to a new building was completed in 2008, which underlined that it was going to take much more than a fiery inferno to halt the historic and award-winning advance of G&J.

And in September 2014 the company illustrated that innovation was part of their game plan when they launched Greenall's Sloe Gin and Greenall's Wild Berry Gin – the first additions to the range for over 250 years.

No wonder the heritage and history of the distillery has been laid out in *G&J Greenall – A Spirited Story Of Gin And Genius*, a neat book by Richard Barnett and Violetta Ruiz Cuenca.

The output of the distillery is titanic...G&J Distillers currently produces 75 different gin recipes for customers.

sloe gin is the perfect blend of balanced botanicals."

Opihr Oriental Spiced Gin is firmly rooted in the ancient Spice Route. Traditionally merchants would travel thousands of miles along the route, trading exotic spices and botanicals from distant lands.

Opihr's hand-picked botanicals epitomise the exotic intensity of the Orient with spicy cubeb berries from Indonesia, black pepper from India and coriander from Morocco. Opihr is a legendary region famed for its wealth and riches which prospered during the reign of King Solomon. The King regularly received cargoes of gold, silver and spices from Opihr and while its exact location remains a mystery, it is thought to have been in the Orient, along the ancient Spice Route.

Tasting Notes: "Soft camphor, sweetness and oriental spices create a warm mouth feel that lingers, with soft cracked black pepper and spice on the finish."

Sloe BLOOM Gin is a seasonal edition that uses hand-picked sloe berries steeped in the highest quality Bloom Gin, distilled in a traditional copper pot still. The sloe berries are macerated in the spirit giving a richly coloured, delicious twist to the floral gin which can be drunk neat, on the rocks or as an ingredient in cocktails.

Tasting Notes: "Appearance: a rich ruby red colour. Nose: a subtle aroma of almonds and kirsch, blended with the light floral aroma of Bloom London Dry Gin. Taste: smooth opening, classical sloe taste, rounded off with some sweetness."

Picture: © Jason Lock Photography.

The stills.

The Master Distiller then adjusts this spirit to ensure that it delivers the perfect strength, taste and quality for Greenall's The Original London Dry Gin.

Greenall's BLOOM Gin had its beginnings when the current Master Distiller Joanne Moore wondered whether the flavours in her camomile tea might work within a gin.

Joanne's experiments led to BLOOM, a light, delicate and floral gin with a slightly sweet taste created by a bespoke blend of three botanicals...honeysuckle, French chamomile and Chinese pomelo...that are used with juniper.

Berkeley Square London Dry Gin is described as the 'single malt' of the gin world.

Two hundred and fifty years of dedication, expertise and craftsmanship have gone into the making of Berkeley Square to craft a complex and refined gin of exceptional quality.

It is distilled in a traditional pot still and infused using the distillery's 'bouquet garni' distillation method, with a blend of hand-picked botanicals, including basil, lavender and kaffir lime leaves.

The water used in Berkeley Square mainly comes from the ancient Triassic pebble beds of the Cheshire Plain, which stretches from the Welsh borders to the foothills of the Pennines.

Only the purest water, filtered through the pebble beds is used to make Berkeley Square, resulting in a clean, pure taste. The region is widely considered to be one of the country's most scenic areas and produces some of the purest water in Britain.

On day one of the distillation process the four core natural botanicals...juniper, coriander, angelica and cubeb berries, are placed by hand in copper pot still No. 8 along with the kaffir lime leaves.

The remaining three botanicals of lavender, sage and basil are wrapped in fine cotton muslin and immersed in the triple distilled spirit to infuse their essential oils.

This unique technique is called the 'bouquet garni' and is a traditional way of cooking used by chefs around the world.

Telephone: +44 (0) 1925 286400
Email: info@quintessentialbrands.com

Using traditional copper stills, it produced 11.2 million litres of alcohol of gin between 1 April 2012 and 31 March 2013.

During the same period 21.5 million litres of vodka was produced.

G&J's own label gins are...

Greenall's The Original London Dry Gin which features eight botanicals, including juniper, coriander, liquorice, orris, angelica, lemon peel, cassia bark and bitter almonds.

Greenall's The Original London Dry Gin is distilled according to traditional methods that go back more than 250 years.

Before the distillation starts, the botanicals are added by hand to the copper still.

This contains a mix of still grain neutral spirit and water sourced from the foothills of the Cheshire Plains.

The botanicals are then allowed to rest and infuse with the spirit.

Using steam, the liquid is heated until it vaporises, taking in all the essential oils and aromas of the botanicals.

The vapour is collected, cooled and condensed to produce a concentrated spirit.

Only the hearts of the distillate is chosen to create the gin. Any residual liquids called 'the heads and tails' (created at the beginning and end of the process) are discarded.

Joanne Moore, Master Distiller of G&J Distillers, part of the international spirits group Quintessential Brands, is truly a master of her craft. Joanne acts as the custodian of the Quintessential Brands portfolio and brand developer for their new products. Joanne is the first female Master Gin Distiller in the world. She is responsible for the creation of three international gins: BLOOM, Berkeley Square London Dry and Opihr Oriental Spiced Gin and for the distillation of Greenall's Original Gin as well as a number of other brands. Joanne is the Master Distiller for over 40% of gin produced in the UK and 20% of all quality gin worldwide. She ensures ongoing accolades and success for G&J Distillers, England's oldest active gin and vodka distillers.

The two new Greenall's Sloe and Wild Berry expressions launched in 2014 – new Greenall's expressions for the first time in 250 years.

33

Gordon's

www.gordons-gin.co.uk

Diageo, which was formed in 1997 by the merger of Guinness and Grand Metropolitan, is the world's largest producer of spirits. It is also one of the major players in the world of wine and beer.

The company's name by the way comes from 'Dies', which is Latin for day, and the Greek "Geo' which means world and the combination of these ancient tongues suggests giving pleasure every day, everywhere.

Diageo sells its brands in more than 180 countries.

Among the multitude of brands that come under the Diageo umbrella are Johnnie Walker, the world's best selling blended Scotch whisky; Smirnoff, the world's best selling vodka and Guinness, the world's best selling stout.

The Diageo gins are Gordon's, which is the world's best selling premium gin, and Tanqueray, the leading imported gin in the USA.

The story of the Diageo gins is one of the oldest in the gin world.

The founding father of Gordon's was Alexander Gordon, who was born in London but whose family had a rich Scottish heritage.

That historic element is carried on in Gordon's to this day...in the shape of the boar's head that appears on every bottle of the gin.

Why a boar? Legend has it that way back in the mists of time a member of the Gordon clan saved the life of the King of Scotland when he was attacked by a wild boar during a royal hunt.

As a reward for his bravery that Gordon was allowed to have a boar's head on his coat of arms.

Fast forward a few centuries and you arrive around the middle of the 18th century, when Alexander Gordon was about to create one of the world's best known gins.

Gordon aimed high, right from the very beginning, as he decided that in the making of the alcohol he would source the finest possible ingredients.

His aim was to produce an unsweetened, gin worthy of the highest table and the finest occasion.

While remaining true to juniper, the keynote ingredient that gave gin its name, Gordon, who founded his world famous distillery in London's Southwark district, believed that success lay in the perfect combination of pure distilled grain spirit and rich botanicals.

Goswell Road in 1910.

Tasting Notes

The strength of the juniper gives Gordon's the classic gin taste. Recipe includes coriander seeds, angelica root, liquorice, orris root, orange and lemon peel. Coriander gives the dry and citrus taste (rather than lemon or orange peel that gives a blunt and overpowering taste in many other gins). Angelica is the magic ingredient that ties together the other botanicals to give a long and complex flavour.

The Gins

GORDON'S LONDON DRY GIN

Carefully distilled using a secret recipe. The distinctively refreshing taste comes from the finest handpicked juniper berries and a selection of other botanicals. It was because of manufacturing constraints that Gordon's was originally produced in green bottles. That of course is now part of the brand's iconic image.

GORDON'S SLOE GIN

The finest wild sloe berries are taken and steeped gently, before adding Gordon's gin. The result marries the dryness of Gordon's with cassis sweetness – perfect in cocktails, as an alternative G&T, or simply on its own.

GORDON'S WITH A SPOT OF ELDERFLOWER

Gordon's London Dry Gin is combined with the delicate taste of elderflower for a delicious twist on a great British classic. The innovative new blend is ideal for enjoying all-year round, and is best served with tonic and ice. Add two strawberry halves to the mix to bring out its delicate taste.

GORDON'S CRISP CUCUMBER

Winner of the 2013 Blind Taste Test in the Financial Times Weekend Magazine; the subtly crisp, aromatic flavour of cucumber is married with delicious Gordon's London Dry Gin to create Gordon's Crisp Cucumber. Mixed with tonic and ice, it makes for a refreshing addition to any evening.

GORDON'S TIME LINE

Alexander Gordon.

1769 After the 1715 Jacobite Rebellion, Aberdonian George Gordon was said to have left Scotland for London where he is believed to have set up business as a merchant and distiller. His son Alexander Gordon, a Londoner of Scottish descent, opened a Distillery in the Southwark area of London, and set about refining his recipe for a spirit named "Gordon's London Dry Gin". Gordon married his cousin Susannah and they had 10 children.

1786 Alexander Gordon moves operations to Clerkenwell, a district favoured because of the purity and abundance of its waters. By this time Gordon has taken on Malachi Foott as a partner and Gordon & Foott were distilling in Clerkenwell.

1800 Gordon's gin was carried by the British Navy and Merchant Navy as their ships travelled all over the world.

1823 Alexander Gordon dies. His second son Charles Gordon carried on the family business. When Charles died in 1849 control of the business was passed on to his only son, who was also named Charles.

1853 Entries in ledgers record payments by Joseph Franks of Melbourne, for consignments of gin brought by the ships 'Nancy' and 'Rostock', payment being made by the settlers in gold dust.

1888 Charles Gordon retires. The last family link with the company is severed. Eleven years later Gordon dies, today the family connection with the company survives in name only.

1898 Gordon & Co amalgamates with Charles Tanqueray & Co to form Tanqueray Gordon & Co. All production moves to Gordon's Goswell Road site.

1902 J. Digby Maitland becomes one of the first overseas agents for the company, making trips to Canada and the United States.

1904 Gordon's distinctive square faced, green bottle for the home market is introduced.

1906 Gordon's Sloe Gin goes into production. This product is considered the most durable of all the cordials produced by the company.

1924 Gordon's is awarded its first Royal Warrant by The Prince of Wales.

1929 Gordon's introduce Orange Gin, which is awarded the Royal Warrant to HRH Prince of Wales.

1931 Gordon's increase their Shaker Cocktail Range with the introduction of Rose, Paradise and Gimlet. Gordon's introduce Lemon Gin, which is awarded the Royal Warrant to HRH Prince of Wales.

1934 Gordon's opens its first distillery in the USA, at Linden, New Jersey.

1941 Gordon's Gin is awarded the Royal Warrant to HM King George VI.

1952 The first Gordon's Distillery in South Africa, at Isando, is opened.

1952 Gordon's Gin is awarded the Royal Warrant to HM Queen Elizabeth II.

1966 The Distillers Company opens its Plainfield Distillery in Illinois, USA. This becomes the thirteenth plant throughout the world, producing Gordon's Gin.

1998 United Distillers and Vintners concentrate all UK spirits production in Scotland. Cameronbridge in Fife, is now the centre for the production of Gordon's brands. Gordon's wins the Gold medal at the Monde, for both Home and Export Gin. Gordon's Gin (Export) wins Gold at the IWSC and Gordon's Gin (Home) wins Silver.

2002 Gordon's undergo a significant bottle re-design undertaken by brand consultancy Design Bridge. The bottle has a new D-shaped cross section, has taller proportions and embossing on the back and the front.

2006 100th anniversary of Gordon's Sloe Gin.

2011 Gordon's Gin launches a new campaign in the UK. "Shall We G&T Started?" features Emilia Fox and Phillip Glenister.

A UK advert from the 1950s.

A US advert from 1937.

So Gordon laid the foundations for the creation of the style of gin for which the English became renowned.

Those standards that were established by Gordon all those years ago have been maintained right up to today.

And so Gordon's remains a gin that is triple distilled to guarantee the purity of the gin.

Three thousand botanicals are nosed every year in the search to re-create the perfect Gordon's blend.

The juniper berries are carefully chosen from the pick of the annual crop. They are gathered by hand, gently shaken from the tree and then stored for two years.

The patience involved in this part of the process has its rewards since the storage period means that the oils are intensified and the juniper flavours are mellowed.

Gordon's proud boast is that it is the strength of the juniper that gives the gin its classic taste.

The Gordon's recipe also includes coriander seeds, angelica root, liquorice, orris root, orange and lemon peel.

However, the exact blend of the botanicals has remained a closely guarded secret.

A Gordon's van and driver, UK, c.1920.

Harrington Gin

Warner Edwards Distillery,
Falls Farm, 34 High Street,
Harrington NN6 9NU.

Hopefully Queen Victoria might have been amused by the convoluted role that her garden has played in the making of the latest product from this Northamptonshire distillery.

After just about a year in the gin trade, Warner Edwards – which was formed by friends Tom Warner and Sion Edwards – decided to try something different.

This turned out to be Victoria's Rhubarb Gin. It's so called because the rhubarb they use has gone from Queen Victoria's garden at Buckingham Palace to Dublin and now to a farm on Crown Estate in Lincolnshire.

According to the distillers the original plant that grew at Buckingham Palace is no longer. So it's only by a remarkable chance that it has found its way back and forth across the Irish Sea.

Warner Edwards stress that the rhubarb in their Victoria Rhubarb Gin – which features another nod to history by including the iconic Penny Black image on its label – has always been grown in the traditional Victorian kitchen farm style.

This renders it free from chemical sprays and artificial fertiliser and this assists the overall flavour.

The basis of the rhubarb flavoured drink is Harrington Dry Gin – which is the gin that started it all for the two friends, who met on their first day of studies at Harper Adams Agricultural College in 1997. Both had farming backgrounds and both had an idea of setting up in the drinks industry.

Originally they thought about making vodka. Instead they settled on gin and with the help of a friend, Heather McAllister – who worked for a flavouring company – they created their first batch of gin in November 2012.

There are 11 botanicals and three of the key botanicals are juniper, coriander and cardamom.

Crucial in achieving the taste they were looking for was the supply of water from a local source that goes back to the time of the Knights Hospitaller.

Their small batch gins, they also make Elderflower Infused (the elderflower is foraged from the farm) and Sloe Gin, are all distilled in Curiosity, a bespoke Arnold Holstein still.

The Warner Edwards Distillery.

Tasting Notes

Harrington Dry Gin: On the nose the quality of the spirit instantly shines through with rich notes of pepper, nutmeg and fresh elderflower. Palate: Due to the one-shot distillation process the spirit is incredibly smooth and full bodied with a deep botanical flavour. Sweet notes of juniper and citrus come through at the start followed by a peppery middle bite and a long warm finish of nutmeg and finally cardamom. The finish is long and spiced due to the amount of essential oils we get through in gin, the flavours wrap around your teeth and palate beautifully.

Curiosity, a bespoke Arnold Holstein still.

The name Curiosity was selected after an incident that sounds as though it might have come from a slapstick comedy.

As the distillery was being built, a new cement floor was put in place. As this was drying, a random cat from the village decided to have a wander, leaving its paw prints right across the floor.

Someone murmured that curiosity killed the cat, but satisfaction brought it back.

And that was that, The team decided that the still just had to be named Curiosity!

Since they started up Warner Edwards have won seven awards, including double gold at the San Francisco World Spirits Competition.

The focus right now is on the gins but there are plans to create a variety of spirits and to make even more use of locally foraged produce.

Telephone: +44 (0) 1536 710623
www.warneredwards.com

Tom Warner and Sion Edwards.

Hendrick's

William Grant & Sons, Girvan Distillery, Grangestone Industrial Estate, Girvan, Ayrshire KA26 9PT.

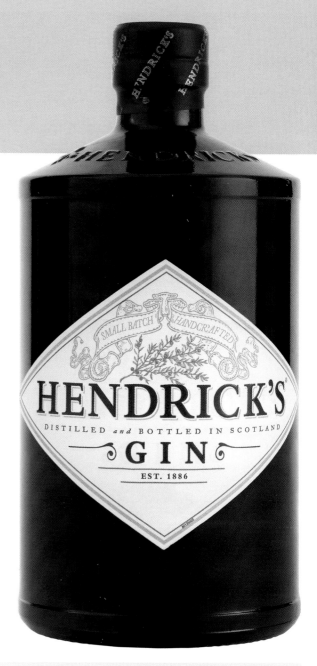

Even the place that provides the water that's used by Hendrick's – famously made with an infusion of cucumber and rose petals that produces a deliciously floral aroma – sounds different.

It is called Penwhapple. Or, to be precise, the Penwhapple Reservoir, that sits between Girvan and Dailly in South Ayrshire, that is the source of the pure, soft water that plays such a vital part in the gin's top secret recipe.

That secrecy, of a distillery which is not open to the public, is not exaggerated since Master Distiller Lesley Gracie is one of only four people privileged to possess the precise details of the Hendrick's recipe.

What is known to folk outwith that very tight circle is that Hendrick's uses 11 botanicals that arrive at Girvan from all over the globe. These are juniper berries, of course, coriander seeds, angelica root, orris root, lemon peel, chamomile, cubeb berries, orange peel, elderflower, yarrow and caraway seeds.

The award-winning, family owned distillery that created Hendrick's was founded by William Grant in 1886.

Today Grant's direct descendants still control the company which also produces whiskies, including famous single malt Glenfiddich and the Balvenie malts as well as Grant's blended whisky. Grants's also make other spirits.

The distillery stands a curling stone's throw from the majestic island of Ailsa Craig, and Hendrick's was born when Charles Gordon – great grandson of William Grant told Lesley Gracie about an 1860 Bennett copper pot still and an 1948 Carter-Head still that he had bought at auction.

These antiques were restored and Ms Gracie started experimenting with botanicals until she came up with the unique creation that is Hendrick's.

Penwhapple Reservoir.

Tasting Notes

"Once the infusions of rose and cucumber are added you will find robust pungent, fruity and citrus flavours derived from juniper, cubeb and orange and lemon peel. There's dryness from angelica and orris, and spiciness from coriander and caraway balanced by fresh, floral, herb and marzipan notes derived from elderflower, meadowsweet, chamomile and rose with cucumber imparting freshness and a delicate sweetness."

The Hendrick's recipe was finalised by Lesley in 1999 and a year later Hendrick's was launched in the American market.

Since then it has spread globally. But despite its international success Hendrick's continues to be handcrafted in small batches of 450 litres at a time.

The philosophy here is that the small batches mean that even more quality control is held by Lesley Gracie and her stillman, Alan Rimmer.

Hendrick's was the first to use a marriage of two spirits – one that has bathed the botanicals and one that has steamed them – created by the three Hendrick's stills.

By boiling the botanicals, both the Bennett and Carrick Stills (identical copper pot stills) produce an identical spirit with great depth of flavour.

Conversely, the Carter-Head Still gently bathes the botanicals in vapour, producing a smooth spirit with subtle flavour characteristics.

Combining the two spirits creates a divinely smooth gin that has both the required character and balance of subtle flavours.

In the making of Hendrick's, a recipe of 11 botanicals is put into the stills – in one still it's added to the spirit / water mix and in the other still it's put in a basket above between the rectifying column and the condenser – and the liquids gently heated.

The 'middle cut' distillate from the stills is collected and blended together. Water is then added to bring the distillate down to bottling strength before the all-important cucumber and rose petal essences are added.

There is a story behind the distinctive Hendrick's bottle. In Victorian times, when the Bennett still was made and William Grant & Sons was formed, precious liquids were placed in dark bottles to protect them from the light.

Accordingly, Hendrick's have just re-used this simple idea, placing the gin into dark apothecary style bottles to ensure the liquid remains in as prime condition as possible.

The final touch to a unique brand involves the roots of Master Distiller Lesley Gracie.

She's the Great, Great, Great... Granddaughter of George Stephenson, the English civil and mechanical engineer who built the first public inter-city railway line in the world to use steam locomotives. His son, Robert Stephenson also created 'Stephenson's Rocket' – the most advanced locomotive of its day in 1829.

When she is not busy creating spirit, she can be found tending to her menagerie of 11 animals, including two tortoises. She also has a collection of 47 orchids, all of which adorn her front room. She also works closely with a valuable team member, the distillery pig Horatio.

Telephone: +44 (0) 208 332 1188
Email: info@wgrant.com

Hendrick's Carter Head Still.

Juniper Green

London & Scottish International,
Bramley, Surrey GU5 oAB.

An independent company owned and operated by the Parker family from Edinburgh, London & Scottish International produces the world's first organic gin. The company is headed by Chief Executive Officer Chris Parker – who has been involved in the international distribution of London Dry Gin for almost 40 years – and managing director Alex Parker who joined the company in 2005 after successfully introducing new major brands to the UK.

They have three gins – Juniper Green Organic Gin – which is the world's first organic gin – Swordsman London Dry Gin and Marlow's London Dry Gin.

Juniper Green Organic Gin, which is reckoned to be the world's first craft gin, was introduced in the UK in 1999 and is now available worldwide.

It is a unique gin which has won 19 international medals.

HRH The Price of Wales first purchased Juniper Green in 2001 and in 2007 the company was honoured to receive his Royal Warrant.

Juniper Green, which is distilled and bottled in London, is the first gin in 50 years to receive a Royal Warrant.

Swordsman London Dry Gin is a classic juniper-based gin, with a distinctive red and white label which is to be found on shelves ranging from sunny California to the vast open spaces of the Urals.

Swordsman, which features the familiar image of a Guardsman on the label, is distilled at London's oldest independent distillery in the diminutive Tom Thumb still.

Marlow's London Dry Gin echoes the famous playwright's London successes and is established in export markets.

Telephone: +44 (0) 1483 894650
Email: office@londonandscottish.co.uk

Tom Thumb and Thumbelina Stills.

Tasting Notes

Juniper Green is juniper-led with a very fresh nose followed by an unmistakeable true gin flavour. The organic spirit is very smooth, allowing a long enjoyable finish.

Swordsman London Distilled Dry Gin is strongly flavoured with juniper.

Marlow's: The underlying hint of coriander lingers on the palate and enhances the enjoyment of this classic London Dry Gin.

London Hill

Ian MacLeod Distillers,
Russell House, Broxburn EH52 5BU.

The Glengoyne Distillery, owned by Ian Macleod Distillers.

London Hill Gin can trace its origins back to 1785 when the site of the current Langley Distillery in the West Midlands was a brewery, known as Langley Crosswells.

Sited over the convergence of three ancient underground springs, it was converted into a gin distillery just before the First World War as the popularity of gin blossomed with the advent of cocktail recipes from the USA.

Gin at Langley Distillery is produced the same way today as it always has been, in copper pot stills, some of which are over one hundred years old, to traditional recipes passed down from one Master Distiller to another.

London Hill Gin production is handled by one particular copper pot still called "Jenny", which was named after one of the original distillery owner's family.

Tasting Notes

Nose: Elegant and balanced, lemon and coriander blend excellently with Juniper. Palate: Delicate to the taste, with different spices and flavours gently appearing one by one. Finish: The complexity continues, leaving the mouth wonderfully refreshed.

Jenny is the largest pot still in Europe, an indication of London Hill Gin's popularity.

Production is overseen by Master Distiller Rob Dorsett who has 35 years of experience.

The precise recipe for London Hill Gin is a closely guarded secret, but its bias is towards citrus tones which comes from the addition of ribbons of citrus peels, including lemon and sweet orange. Together with these citrus peels, a subtle blend of other botanicals sourced from all over the world is used...juniper berries from Italy and the Balkans, Bulgarian coriander, cassia bark from China, Madagascan cinnamon, angelica root from northern France and Belgium, as well as orris root and liquorice from Italy.

The process begins when the neutral grain-based alcohol is charged into the pot still at 96% ABV. Here, it is reduced with water to about 57% ABV before a combination of botanicals is added.

The mixture is then left to macerate overnight, which helps to extract the special flavours and characteristics.

Next, the still is heated using a steam jacket to extract essential oils from the botanicals.

These are what give the spirit its flavour. The first distillate 'runnings' are re-circulated until an appropriate standard and strength (over 90% ABV) is reached.

The lower quality, early part of the run ('foreshots') and end of the run ('feints'), as judged by the skill and experience of the 'Stillman', are run off to be redistilled.

Only the 'middle run' is used to produce London Hill Gin. This is run off at about 80-85% ABV.

Finally, the resulting concentrate is blended with alcohol to produce a high strength gin at over 90% ABV, which is then reduced with water to the required strength.

London Hill Gin has won a hat trick of gold medals at the annual International Wine & Spirit Competition.

It is part of the portfolio of Ian Macleod Distillers, a family owned company, which includes among its brands Glengoyne, Tamdhu, Isle of Skye and Smokehead Scotch whiskies.

Telephone: +44 (0)1506 852205
Email: info@ianmacleod.com

Makar Glasgow Gin

Glasgow Distillery Company Ltd,
234 West George Street,
Glasgow G2 4QY.

H istory is being made in a warehouse on an industrial estate that lies between Glasgow's city centre and the airport. It's here that for the first time in over 100 years a Glasgow distillery is in operation.

And, after almost three years in the planning, it is producing Makar Glasgow Gin, the first gin to be made in Glasgow.

Makar, which is a Scots word that means poet or bard, is a name that has a lyrical ring to it.

And this sense of poetry seems to have touched Scots poet and dramatist, Liz Lochhead who in 2011 was named the second Scots Makar, or national poet.

Liz has visited the distillery and promises to write a poem in praise of Annie, which is the name of the copper pot still that is used in the making of Makar.

The roots of Makar Glasgow Gin are freshly planted – production of the gin started in late September 2014 – but the inspiration for the distillery goes back to the 18th Century.

Founded in 1770, the original distillery became known as The Glasgow Distillery in 1825 and continued to function until 1903.

Since then memories of the Glasgow Distillery had vanished in the mists of time – until the triumvirate of Mike Hayward, Liam Hughes and Ian McDougall came together to create a craft distillery.

And so The Glasgow Distillery Company was reborn and work began on conjuring up the recipe that has become Makar Glasgow Gin.

The threesome took the plunge after a tasting at Sacred Gin in London and seeing what a boutique gin distillery could achieve.

Another member of the Makar Glasgow Gin team is Head Distiller Jack Mayo, a graduate of the International Centre for Brewing & Distilling at Edinburgh's Heriot-Watt University.

Gold dust was struck after many attempts to get the balance of the botanicals right.

The gin, which is distilled a total of seven times to make it smoother, is made in a traditional pot still and a gin basket is used in the top and that is where the more delicate botanicals are placed.

Eight botanicals are included in the recipe...juniper, coriander, angelica, liquorice, cassia, rosemary, lemon peel and black pepper.

Another interesting factor in the process is that the water used in the making of Makar Glasgow

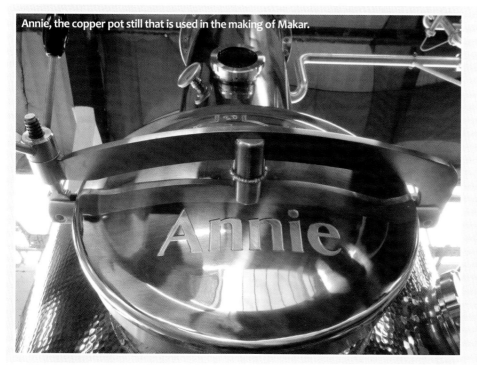
Annie, the copper pot still that is used in the making of Makar.

Tasting Notes

"The Juniper notes give Makar a bright, robust and aromatic perfumed nose with citrus notes and hints of herbaceous rosemary.

On the palate Makar delivers a well-balanced juniper-led flavour sensation with a full rounded mouth feel which leads to a smooth long finish with a hint of the rosemary and spicy black pepper that works fantastically well in a Gin & Tonic and other classic cocktails."

Gin comes from the incredibly soft waters of Loch Katrine, which is the same source as the original 18th Century Glasgow Distillery.

The distillation of the gin takes about eight hours, so the distillery has a current daily capacity of producing 300 bottles of Makar.

And when they describe Makar Glasgow Gin as handcrafted they really mean it. Even the bottle labels have to be applied by hand!

This is because the Makar bottle has a seven-sided shape.

Seven sides were decided on for a variety of reasons. Seven, of course, is a lucky number. Seven is the number of botanicals that are added to juniper, the heart of gin. And of course there are a couple of sevens in 1770, when the first Glasgow Distillery was established.

They decided to name the gin Makar Glasgow Gin after considering and rejecting more than 200 names.

After loads of frustration, they were going through notes of suggested titles when they stumbled across the Scots word Makar and what it meant. Suddenly the distillers had that eureka moment.

Now that Makar Glasgow Gin is underway, there are plans to produce single malt whiskies and to that end a major decision has been made...their whisky stills will be named Tara and Mhari!

Email: info@glasgowdistillery.com

Head Distiller Jack Mayo labelling the bottles by hand.

NB Gin

Legal eagles Steve and Viv Muir knew they wanted to spread their wings into a fresh enterprise. But the issue was exactly with what the married couple – who are both lawyers – might take flight.

An initial notion from Steve was to set up a brewery. But Viv was the sales section of the team and felt that she'd be as useful pitching beer as Steve would be selling handbags!

Back to the drawing board. Then they were struck by the realisation that since they both enjoyed gin and knew a fair bit about the drink, that the solution was obvious...

They'd start making gin. So the pair plunged themselves into researching gin and all things related to it.

Steve bought a batch of botanicals and experimented with mixes and tastes...even on a raw basis.

The next step was like an episode out of TV situation comedy *The Good Life*.

In their kitchen Steve and Viv set up an old pressure cooker and pipes rescued from an old central heating system and steamed the botanicals through this Heath Robinson apparatus, to see how various combinations worked.

After that the couple invested more than £1,000 in a more professional bit of gear...a glass lab still.

They applied for a licence and ran their ginery in the kitchen until they produced the gin that they had been hoping for.

They then set the wheels in motion and instructed the build of a proper gin still, the design of which had to be aligned to the taste they wanted to create, so it took months of detailed planning. It was custom built in London by the oldest still makers in the world, and in August 2013, was finally installed in the Muirs' new micro-distillery in North Berwick.

Key to it all, as with every gin making, was achieving quality and consistency.

Steve and Viv were ruthless. If the distilling went even a minute over the allotted time the gin was dumped.

"It would still have been a high quality gin but not precisely the gin that we wanted to make," explains Viv.

"We would lose money rather than make something that wasn't right on the button."

Since they began production in October 2013 the Muirs have steadfastly only made small batches of NB Gin.

NB Gin is always distilled in batches of less than 100 litres.

Tasting Notes

"*An unmistakable aroma of juniper invites you into the glass. Each botanical is revealed with startling clarity. A burst of clean citrus is followed by warm earthy notes and a dash of pepper spice is complemented by subtle zests of orange. All are rounded off with a final flourish of juniper.*

"*The Palate is completely aligned with the Nose. Unmistakeable juniper flavours are well balanced with citrus freshness, warm earthy flavours and a pinch of white pepper. An amazing smooth texture fills the mouth finishing with a warming juniper flavour. Extremely persistent but clean, fresh with a wonderful texture.*"

Small batches typically means 100 litres or fewer and NB Gin is always distilled in batches of less than 100 litres.

It is handmade in North Berwick from pure grain spirit and carefully selected botanicals to produce a full flavoured quality gin.

They celebrated the first anniversary of the boutique micro-distillery by producing a very limited navy strength edition – just 99 bottles.

But the award-winning NB have no intention of creating a series of recipes. Viv is adamant that they will only ever make NB Gin and adds that the limited navy strength gin was created from the same recipe.

As well as its UK outlets, NB is sold in Germany, Denmark and Spain and has plans to spread further into Europe and the USA.

Telephone: +44 (0) 845 467 4547
Email: info@nbgin.co.uk

NB GIN COCKTAILS

FRENCH 39
A modern Scottish twist on a classic invented in Harry's Bar in Paris in 1915. The concoction was said to be so powerful it was like being shot by the French 75 – a 75mm machine gun used by the French in WWII.

Ingredients:
1 white sugar cube
2 dashes home-made lavender bitters
25ml NB Gin
Top with Champagne

Method:
Build in order of recipe in chilled champagne flute

Garnish: A pear slice

ALL ABOVE THE BORDER
A fine blend of Scottish Gin, Scottish Whisky and Scottish raspberries.

Ingredients:
40ml NB Gin
12.5ml Glenkinchie Whisky
20ml raspberry syrup

Method:
Stir down and serve in a chilled cocktail glass.

LAVENDER LADY
A classic dry White Lady, softened with lavender syrup for the modern day palate.

Ingredients:
37.5ml NB Gin
12.5ml Cointreau/Triple Sec
25ml fresh lemon juice
12.5ml lavender syrup

Method:
Shake and serve in chilled cocktail glass.

THE NB FIZZ
Ingredients:
2 shots NB
1 shot freshly squeezed lemon juice
1/2 shot sugar syrup
Soda

Method:
Shake the first three ingredients with ice and strain into a chilled glass. Then top up with soda.

I exercise strong self control.
I never drink anything stronger
than gin before breakfast.
– *W.C. Fields, film star*

One martini is just right,
two is too many,
three is not enough.
– *James Thurber,*
cartoonist, author,
journalist, playwright

They all thought she was dead;
but my father he kept ladling
gin down her throat till
she came to so sudden that she
bit the bowl off the spoon.
– *George Bernard Shaw,*
playwright, Pygmalion

No. 3 London Dry Gin

Berry Bros & Rudd, No. 3 St James's Street, London SW1A 1EG.

Lord Byron, one of the greatest British poets, the 18th Prime Minister William Pitt, Napoleon III and the Aga Khan are just four of the famous customers of celebrated London wine and spirits merchants Berry Bros & Rudd.

Impressively, the company – which has been in business since 1698 – is also the Queen's wine and spirits merchant and it has had a royal connection since the reign of George III, when the company began supplying the Royal Family.

A number of wines and spirits are sold under the company's own label and in 1923 it created Cutty Sark whisky.

When Britain's oldest wine and spirits merchant produced No. 3 London Dry Gin it was named after their home in St. James's Street and it also celebrated the merchant's three centuries of heritage. Additionally, the number marks the use of three fruits and three spices – the botanicals which flavour No. 3 London Dry Gin.

For those interested in numerology, a fascinating coincidence can also be noted that when Berry's commissioned experts to help create their gin, the team comprised THREE men and THREE women! This team was headed by Dr David Clutton, the holder of the world's only PhD in gin flavour.

A year was spent seeking the right recipe and Dr Clutton's team operated under the remit to make No. 3 taste 'as gin should' – without the use of an excessive amount of ingredients and distilled in traditional copper pot stills without any over-elaboration.

So, with classic simplicity the goal, the experts placed a robust helping of juniper at the heart of No. 3. This was then complemented by five more botanicals – sweet Spanish orange peel, grapefruit peel, angelica root, Moroccan coriander and cardamom seeds.

By going against the trend for a multitude of botanicals, the creators felt that they were going back towards a more traditional dry gin.

No. 3 London Dry Gin, which chairman Simon Berry describes as 'unmistakably traditional' is bottled in a distinctive, high-shouldered green bottle with a key set into its glass.

The key is yet another nod to the history and legacy of Berry Bros & Rudd.

It is a symbol of the traditions and secrets within the company's history and is modelled on the key that was used to open the company's inner sanctum...the door of 'The Parlour' – one of the oldest rooms in the Berry Bros & Rudd shop.

www.no.3gin.com

The Berry Bros & Rudd Shop at No. 3 St James's Street.

Tasting Notes

"Nose: Bright, crisp and fresh with an uplifting welcome of juniper. Palate: Juniper to the fore, supported by floral, summery notes and spicy, warm flavours of cardamom. There is plenty of citrus zing: grapefruit and sweet orange contribute a sharp fruitiness, complimented by the soft gingery spiciness of coriander. Finish: The earthy dryness of angelica kicks in."

Pickering's

Summerhall Distillery, Summerhall, Edinburgh EH9 1PL.

Pickering's Gin has its exotic beginnings outlined on a very special scrap of paper, now framed. It's a note that was hand-written in Bombay in 1947 when a friend of Marcus Pickering's father devised a recipe for gin.

The scribble was given to the late Mr Pickering and then handed down to Marcus who, more than 65 years on from the recipe first being penned, decided to put it to use.

Marcus and his business partner, Matt Gammell, launched their company on March 27, 2014 – two and a half years after Marcus first came up with the idea of establishing a gin distillery.

They have based the distillery in a building that was once the veterinary school of Edinburgh University.

And it is there that they have finessed the Bombay recipe, tweaking it for the contemporary palate.

There are nine botanicals used – juniper, coriander, cardamom, angelica, fennel, anise, lemon, lime and cloves.

These are all carefully measured and added to the grain spirit in a 500 litre copper still which is named Gert.

Pickering's explain that the secret of the gin's smoothness is Gert's custom-designed bain marie heating system, which provides a gentle all-over-heat to the still.

This means that the botanicals have what Pickering's term a 'luxurious' simmer that coaxes out their subtle, soft flavours.

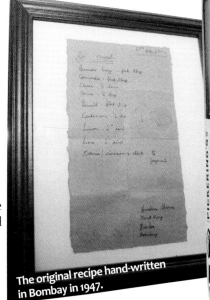

The original recipe hand-written in Bombay in 1947.

As well as classic Pickering's Gin they have made a limited edition (500 bottles) navy strength gin to celebrate becoming the official gin of the Royal Edinburgh Military Tattoo.

Pickering's Gin has nine botanicals.

Tasting Notes

"NOSE: Clean fresh pine derived from the juniper, with citrus notes.

TASTE: Strongly aromatic in the mouth. There are hints of liquorice and cinnamon, slightly nutty notes and a sweet lavender-like softness.

FINISH: Refreshingly crisp and dry."

Matt in the Royal Dick Bar.

Next door to the distillery is The Royal Dick bar, which used to be where the veterinary hospital's operating theatre was.

And in the Royal Dick you can experience Pickering's on tap!

That is because of an ingenious system whereby Pickering's Gin is piped from a pressurised tank in the distillery directly into the bar where it is served on draught!

In keeping with a slight touch of eccentricity is the fact that the bottles of Pickering's Gin are neither round nor square; which means they have a striking look.

But the bottle shape created a problem because there isn't a standard labelling machine that can be used for the Pickering's bottles. So the company created their own labelling machine to do the job.

Another neat touch is the 1964 Austin 35 van in Pickering's distinctive red and cream livery which is used to deliver the gin.

The team at Pickering's welcome visitors for tours that show how the hand crafted, small batch gin is made.

Telephone: +44 (0) 131 290 2901
Email: enquiries@pickeringsgin.com

Marcus and the 500 litre copper still which is named Gert.

Pictures: Alistair Devine.

Sacred Gin

Sacred Spirits Co., 5 Talbot Road, Highgate, London N6 4QS.

Schoolboy Latin came in handy for Ian Hart as he turned to the past to help decide his future. Co-founder of the nation's most unusual distillery – it is set in the rear lounge of his Victorian home in Highgate, London – Ian studied papers from the 16th Century spice trade as he embarked on the painstaking search for a unique, hand-crafted gin.

Eventually he came up with a recipe that was loosely based on a 17th Century formula and involved the use of 12 organically sourced botanicals.

These included Tuscan juniper, whole Spanish citrus fruits (pith, peel and juice), Indian coriander, cardamom from Guatemala, Italian orris and Spanish liquorice.

The final botanical flourish was Boswellia Sacra – that's the Latin name of course but its better known to me and you as Frankincense!

This use of Boswellia Sacra, and since Frankincense also had an obvious connection with the Gospels, meant there could only be one name for the company…Sacred Spirits!

When Ian, and his partner, Hilary Whitney, created the company in 2008 they were making history by setting up the only home distillery in London.

Changed days of course, because 300 years ago it's reckoned that there were more than 1,500 home distilleries in London!

Creating a multiple award-winning gin happened after Ian, who had been a Wall Street trader and a City head-hunter, found himself out of work in 2006.

"I decided then to try and make something," remembers Ian.

Quite what he was going to make was not decided. Initially, his imagination was let loose on the scientific world. He taught himself microwave engineering and dabbled with variations on Nikola Tesla's idea of transmitting electricity through air.

There were some experiments with Bordeaux – Ian has been a wine collector since he was 18 – by distilling the wine to make it richer, before he turned his thoughts towards gin.

Gin-making was not an overnight success story. Ian came up with 23 different recipes before hitting pay dirt.

Each of his attempts were tasted by willing guinea pigs at his local, The Wrestlers. Then on the night of the 23rd test, Ian knew that he had finally created what he'd been striving for.

"The landlord of my local pub said if that gin was bottled he would certainly sell it," says Ian.

And so Sacred Gin was born.

Tasting Notes

Sacred Gin "Crystal clear. Lush, pine-fresh juniper nose, delicate violet flowers, crushed cardamom pods and cinnamon. Long zesty finish with lingering pine and peppercorns."

Sacred Juniper Gin "Crystal clear. Fresh, clean, 'slightly green', pine forest nose with white pepper spice. Lingering dill with black pepper spice."

Sacred Coriander Gin "A spicy classic gin with dominant notes of Indian coriander seeds to create a unique dry spirit with an uplifting and aromatic bouquet."

Sacred Cardamom Gin "Crystal clear. Fabulously aromatic crushed cardamom nose with pine freshness and slightly cracked black pepper. Clean, strangely sweet, invigorating full-flavoured cardamom palate with black pepper spice and faint aniseed flavours. Extremely, long, fresh cardamom finish."

Sacred Pink Grapefruit Gin "Crystal clear. Subdued, clean nose with grainy peppery spirit aromas as evident as sweet, delicately fruit grapefruit. Delicate sweet pink grapefruit flavours fight for attention on a peppery spiced palate. Cracked black pepper and citrusy grapefruit alternatively features in the long fresh finish."

Sacred Orris Gin "Not surprisingly, orris has a floral character, reminiscent of Parma Violets – perhaps the olfactory equivalent of the colour purple."

The nation's most unusual distillery.

From the very start it was clear that Ian Hart was going to make a different gin. Most gins are distilled in copper pots but Ian opted for a vacuum distilled process under glass.

Ian has five bespoke stills – all designed to his own specifications and made especially for him by a glassware manufacturer.

Using this vacuum method means air is sucked out of the glassware with a vacuum pump – which is kept in an old Wendy House in Ian's garden – to reduce pressure so that distillation occurs at a much lower temperature than traditional pot stills.

This produces fresher, lusher distillates. Ian reckons that the perfect example of this comes when you think of the marmalade flavour of cooked oranges versus fresh cut oranges.

The organically sourced botanicals are macerated separately for four to six weeks at the minimum, with no air contact, in English wheat spirit at 50% ABV.

This is a VERY LONG time since it is more common for an overnight maceration to be adopted.

Ian decided on a more slow and painstaking approach because he felt it would result in having a greater freshness of the botanicals.

All the macerated botanicals are also distilled separately so they retain all of their individual character and depth.

They are then blended to create Sacred Gin. Every bottle of Sacred Gin is hand-distilled by Ian and each bottle is individually numbered.

Ian has five bespoke stills.

And the demanding process carried out by Ian has had very positive feedback.

Sacred Gin was awarded a Double Gold Medal at the San Francisco World Spirits Competition, first prize for Best Gins with Tonic by the Craft Distillers Association, and it received the Palate Pleaser Award from Spears Design for Living Awards in conjunction with Harrods in 2011.

In addition, Sacred Gin was the overall winner of the Micro distilleries Ginmasters, 2009.

And there's more bubbling away in Ian Hart's back room.

Other products that he has created include...Sacred Cardamom Gin, Sacred Pink Grapefruit Gin, Sacred London Dry Vodka, Sacred Organic Vodka, Sacred Spiced English Vermouth, made with English wine, and Sacred Rose Hip Cup – the English alternative to Campari.

When he chatted with the author, Ian was awaiting the completion of a batch of a Christmas Pudding Gin which he has based on a Christmas pudding recipe handed down by his Great Aunt Nellie!

Today Ian and Hilary's cottage industry produces 30,000 bottles a year. Apart from the UK sales, they export to 17 countries.

He's proud of the achievements and that the example of Sacred Spirits has shown other would-be gin makers what can be done.

No wonder Ian says that he's never been happier!

Telephone: +44 (0) 208 340 0992
Email: info@sacredspiritscompany.com

Shetland Reel

Shetland Distillery Company, Unst, Shetland ZE2 9EF.

Scotland's most remote and northerly gin distillery had humble beginnings...in the kitchen of Stuart Nickerson's home in Portknockie, a village on the Moray Firth.

A veteran of the whisky industry – with William Grant and the Girvan Distillery – Stuart had the dream of establishing a gin distillery in Shetland.

To that end he teamed up with Grantown-on-Spey based entrepreneur Frank Strang and they went into partnership to create a boutique style gin.

But before getting the first commercial distillation of gin in Shetland off the ground, Stuart had to work out his recipe.

Which is why he got an Excise licence to have a laboratory-sized still – 5 litre capacity – set up in his kitchen.

There then followed a couple of months of trial and error until he was satisfied that he had created a traditional style gin that incorporated specific elements of Shetland.

What Stuart came up with was a gin that possessed a significant difference – apple mint, which is grown and harvested on Unst, a remote island that is only accessible from the Shetland mainland via two ferry journeys, via the island of Yell.

The name Shetland Reel reflects the long-time interest in music in the Shetlands. Continuing that link, American Emmy Award winning, country singer/songwriter Jim Salestrom – who is a member of Dolly Parton's band – has written a song about Shetland Reel Gin.

Visitors are encouraged to take in the Shetland Reel Gin experience, to make their own gin and have it bottled on the premises.

The remote nature of the Unst distillery means that a visit is a unique two day adventure. It includes being collected at the airport before being ferried to the island of Yell and then boarding another ferry to Unst and then north to Saxa Vord and the distillery.

At the distillery there is a tour that incorporates gin-making and on Day 2 there is the process of bottling and labelling your own gin before receiving a certificate of completion.

Telephone: +44 (0) 1957 711 711   Email: stuart@shetlandreelgin.com

The 100 litre capacity gin still.

Tasting Notes

"Colour: Clear. Nose: Juniper, mixed spices, mixed citrus. Palate: Juniper, mixed spice, sweetness with a citrus tang and a refreshing hint of mint at the end. Finish: Clean and fresh."

Strathearn Distillery

Methven, Perthshire PH1 3QX.

S et in the rural splendour of Perthshire, Strathearn Distillery, which is Scotland's smallest malt whisky distillery is also a creator of a quartet of hand-crafted Gins. These are Classic Gin, Heather and Rose Gin, Oaked Highland Gin and Homecoming Scotland 2014 Gin.

It was in the Spring of 2013 that work began on the renovation of semi-derelict farm buildings and by August/September the first Gins were being produced.

The distillery's philosophy is to recreate Scotland's heritage and history of farm distilling from the 1700's by using traditional methods and materials.

Strathearn, which is headed by David Lang and Tony Reeman-Clark who share previous experience in the drinks trade, produces small batches of premium gin using natural botanicals.

These include juniper, of course, coriander, liquorice root and other flavourings.

The Stills.

The Oaked Highland is perhaps the most intriguing Gin since it includes elements of whisky which are introduced to the Gin via a secret recipe – part of which involves infusing elements from used USA whisky barrels!

Strathearn claim that their Classic Gin – which is a citrus gin based on the Old London Gin Standard – comes with a new twist since it possesses a vibrant hint of the East.

The Heather and Rose Gin is a fragrant drink, a champagne gin, which turns a delicate pink and a waft of Rose scent is released when tonic water is added.

Commissioned by Visit Scotland, to commemorate the year of 2014, the Homecoming Scotland 2014 Gin lives up to its tartan image as it features a mix of Thistle, Heather and other botanicals.

Telephone: +44 (0) 1738 840 100
Email: Info@StrathearnDistillery.com

Strathearn Distillery.

Tasting Notes

Classic Gin – "With its added elements of zest, herbs and spices, it will transport you somewhere between the Southern Mediterranean with its Italian lemons and Spanish grapefruit, or much further East as you detect the hint of kaffir lime leaves and star anise. The taste of summer holidays and relaxing with friends."

Heather and Rose Gin – "The combination of Rose and Heather give very light floral notes and a champagne character. The colour reflects the fields of heather on Scottish hillsides. Floral and light, sweet yet spicy."

Oaked Highland Gin – "With its juniper notes and hints of citrus accented by vanilla this is a gin with a subtle smokiness. A deep golden colour helps to provide the disguise."

Homecoming Scotland 2014 Gin – "A smooth hand-crafted gin, reminiscent of love hearts and sherbet dip. A delicate balance of floral and smooth creamy notes with a hint of citrus zest."

Tanqueray

www.tanqueray.com

Like Gordon's, Tanqueray holds on to a long and illustrious history. The Tanqueray and Willaume families were Huguenots, persecuted members of the French Protestant Church, who fled their country. A consequence of the years of persecution was the St. Bartholomew's Day Massacre of 1572, when Catholics killed thousands of Huguenots in Paris. It is reckoned that more than 50,000 Huguenots eventually crossed the Channel and arrived in Britain.

They were skilled silversmiths and goldsmiths, whose art could be traced back centuries.

By the late 17th century David Willaume had set up business in England, having established himself as a goldsmith in Charing Cross, London.

Just a few years later – by 1719 – he had expanded into banking and then settled into retirement as the owner of the manor of Tingrith in Bedfordshire.

Willaume's daughter, Anne – who was also a gifted goldsmith – married David Tanqueray in 1717.

Tanqueray was such a successful goldsmith that he was recorded as 'Subordinate Goldsmith' to King George II.

The Tanquerays were also men of the cloth and three generations were rectors of the parish of Tingrith...serving a total of devotion to the church there of more than 130 years.

Today the old Rectory at Tingrith is named Tanqueray House and during World War II it was the headquarters for General Charles de Gaulle's Free French movement.

It was Charles Tanqueray who in the early 19th century broke with the tradition of joining the clergy and instead began to experiment with distilling a quality gin at his Bloomsbury distillery, which he and his younger brother John had bought for £6,300.

THE TANQUERAY BOTTLE
THE classic look of the bottle of Tanqueray Gin is inspired by the shape of a cocktail shaker and has been the instantly recognisable design since 1948.

Tasting Notes

TANQUERAY LONDON DRY GIN
• *Tanqueray London Dry Gin is one of the world's most awarded gins with a balanced, multi-layered combination of botanicals:*
> • *Refreshing juniper*
> • *Peppery coriander*
> • *Aromatic angelica*
> • *Sweet liquorice*

• *A four step distillation process is involved in the making of Tanqueray London Dry Gin. The only flavours you will get after the distillation are those of the botanicals and you should get no flavour from the neutral spirit, only strength.*

• *Tanqueray London Dry Gin has a flavour that shines through in sophisticated cocktails and vibrant gin and tonics.*

TANQUERAY NO. TEN™
• *The heart of Tanqueray® No. TEN™ Gin is made by distilling fresh oranges, limes and grapefruit, giving the gin a hint of fresh citrus flavour.*

• *Chamomile flowers create the signature velvety mouth feel and other hand-selected, meticulously sourced botanicals provide further layers of unrivalled taste:*
> • *Refreshing juniper*
> • *Peppery coriander*
> • *Aromatic angelica*
> • *Sweet liquorice*
> • *Oranges*
> • *Limes*
> • *Grapefruit*

• *Tanqueray No. TEN is made in small batches, using only the highest quality distillate, resulting*

Tanqueray advert, US, 1960s.

If this were an ordinary gin, we would have put it in an ordinary gin bottle. *Charles Tanqueray*

"The Tanqueray people said they needed a sophisticated, dignified spokesman. Clearly, they're unaware of Mr. Jenkins' little incident at the Pelican Room."

How refreshingly distinctive.

Tanqueray advert, US, 1994.

The Tanqueray and Gordon families were connected by marriage in 1837 when Susan Gordon, the granddaughter of Alexander Gordon wed Edward Tanqueray, the elder brother of Charles Tanqueray.

But it was not until 1898 that Gordon & Co. and Charles Tanqueray & Co. merged. This was after Charles Gordon, grandson of the founder had in 1878 sold Gordon & Co. to another distiller named John Currie & Co.

The company became Tanqueray Gordon & Co. and in 1922 they joined the Distillers Company.

During the Blitz the London distillery, warehouses and offices were destroyed by German bombs and a new distillery was built near to the original Goswell Road site in 1957.

By the 1980s it was evident that new, bigger premises were required to cope with demand. So a three year plan began to create, on a 26 acre site, a multi-million pound blending,

in a very smooth finish.

TANQUERAY RANGPUR GIN

• *Tanqueray Rangpur Gin takes its name from the Rangpur lime, a unique fruit of the native Indian Rangpur tree that blends the zestiness of lime and the juiciness of a Mandarin orange.*

• *Distilling the Rangpur lime with other botanicals – including bay leaf, ginger and of course juniper – gives Tanqueray Rangpur Gin a subtle, yet memorably zesty citrus twist that makes it ideal for a classic martini cocktail, a highball, or an invigorating short on the rocks.*

TANQUERAY MALACCA GIN

• *Tanqueray Malacca is a sweet, spicy gin with less juniper emphasis and a stronger fruit palate (most notably grapefruit).*

THE TANQUERAY CREST

The crest was granted to the Reverend Edward Tanqueray in 1838.
Edward combined the single plain pineapple of the Willaume family with two battle-axes.
These weapons recognise the part played by the family in the Third Crusade in Palestine where they fought under King Richard the Lion Heart in 1191.
The family name at this time was spelled Tancrery.
The heraldic pineapple comes from the coat-of-arms bestowed in 1767 on the ancient French Willaume family from whom the Tanqueray's are descended.
The Willaume family crest was "on a mount vert, a pineapple or, stalked and crowned proper".

Bottling Line at Goswell Road, c.1960.

bottling and warehouse operation in Laindon, near Basildon, Essex.

Development has continued and in 1991 a Gin Heritage Centre was opened at the site.

Then history turned full circle. The Gordon family had originally come from Aberdeenshire and the world famous gin empire finally took the high road back to Scotland.

Cameronbridge Distillery – which was founded by the Haig distilling family on the banks of the River Leven in Fife in 1823 – became the centre of production of Gordon's and Tanqueray.

In 1991 there was a £22 million investment in the site and then seven years later United Distillers and Vintners announced a £50 million plan to concentrate all its UK spirits production in Scotland.

So Cameronbridge is now the centre for the production of Gordon's, Tanqueray and Smirnoff Vodka.

TANQUERAY LONDON DRY GIN

The history of Tanqueray spans 180 years and so it is no surprise that it boasts an elegance and sophistication.

It is a crisp, dry gin with a rich juniper flavour and its other botanicals include peppery coriander, angelica and sweet liquorice.

The instantly recognisable bottle contains one of the world's most award winning gins.

A four step distillation is part of the process in the making of Tanqueray London Dry Gin, which means you get no flavour from the neutral spirit, just its strength. The flavour comes from the delicate mix of the botanicals.

TANQUERAY No. TEN

With a new gin comes a new bottle design.

Ten facets flow down the green bottle and meet at the base in the shape of a citrus squeezer.

The shape harks back to the Art Deco era when the cocktail culture was all the rage.

Tanqueray No. Ten is the only gin in the Hall of Fame at the San Francisco World Competition.

A small batch gin, Tanqueray No. Ten is made by distilling fresh oranges, limes and grapefruit to give the gin a hint of fresh citrus flavour.

Chamomile flowers create a velvety feel on the mouth and the other hand selected botanicals are...juniper, coriander, angelica, oranges, limes and grapefruit.

TANQUERAY RANGPUR GIN

The name, as it suggests, is taken from the Rangpur lime in India – a fruit that blends the zest of lime with the juiciness of the Mandarin orange.

The Rangpur lime is distilled with the botanicals – bay leaf, ginger, and juniper, naturally.

The result is a subtle yet zesty citrus twist.

TANQUERAY MALACCA GIN

This is a sweet, spicy gin with less of a juniper emphasis and a palate that is stronger on its fruitiness, most notably grapefruit.

TANQUERAY TIME LINE

Charles Tanqueray, c.1850.

1868 Charles Tanqueray died and his son, Charles Waugh Tanqueray took over the business at the age of 20.

1895 Earliest evidence of Tanqueray Gin in the USA, from a price list from W. A. Taylor & Co. of New York, with an illustration of 'Tanqueray's Finest Old Tom'.

1898 Charles Tanqueray & Co. merged with Gordon & Co. to form Tanqueray Gordon & Co. The company transferred all its production from the Bloomsbury Distillery to Gordon's Goswell Road site.

1912 Earliest bottle of Tanqueray Finest Dry Gin held at the Diageo Archive.

1917 3 May – It was resolved to give a subscription of £1000 to the anti prohibition campaign in the USA.

1925 Tanqueray Gordon & Co. receive their first Royal Warrant from HRH The Prince of Wales.

1948 Tanqueray gin began to be produced in the now familiar green bottle.

1950s/60s James M. McCunn & Co., distributors for Tanqueray gin in the USA, greatly increased the popularity for the gin with a brilliant PR campaign concentrated on California. Celebrities such as Frank Sinatra, Sammy Davis Junior and Bob Hope, were seen to be drinking Tanqueray Gin, in a small restaurant called the "Buena Vista" in San Francisco. In 1962 the brand sold 25,674 cases in the USA, this jumped to 47,000 the following year, without spending a penny on either advertising or promoting the brand.

1979 Tanqueray Gin sold one million cases.

1985 Tanqueray Gin won the Queen's Award for Export Achievement.

1987 Tanqueray Gin was awarded the Gold award for Gin by the International Wine and Spirits Committee in Portugal. Many more awards followed over the years.

1998 UDV concentrate all UK spirits production in Scotland, Cameronbridge in Fife, is now the centre for the production of Tanqueray Gin. Tanqueray Gin won the Gold Medal at the Monde Selection.

2006 Tanqueray sells 2 million cases of Tanqueray Gin and produces a limited edition bottle and box to commemorate the event. Tanqueray launches Tanqueray Rangpur in America.

2009 New Tanqueray Gin pack is launched. Its launch is accompanied by the Global Tanqueray campaign "Resist Simple".

1830s Charles Tanqueray, (1810-1868), son of a Bedfordshire clergyman, sets up the Bloomsbury Distillery in London in 1830. Experimenting over the years with many possible ingredients, Charles Tanqueray finally produced the key balance of ingredients and Tanqueray Gin was launched.

1839 Charles Tanqueray produced a spiced gin. In 1997, inspiration was taken from this liquid, and Tanqueray Malacca Gin was launched.

1847 Tanqueray Gin was making inroads among the spice planters and traders of far-away Jamaica, shown by the recovery of a tall ceramic crock discovered in a shipwreck in Kingston, Jamaica, bearing the legend 'Tanqueray Gin'.

Tarquin's Gin

Southwestern Distillery, Higher Trevibban Farm, St Ervan, Wadebridge, Cornwall PL27 7SH.

Tarquin Leadbetter had embarked on a wide and varied set of pursuits before coming to the conclusion that he had a desire to create gin. Before he was 23 years old he'd studied at famous culinary college, Le Cordon Bleu, worked as a cook in France and earned an Economics degree that got him a job in the City in Emerging Markets.

None of that seemed to satisfy him. So in 2011 he quit London and headed back to the West Country, where he had grown up, and set up a hand crafted distiller in Cornwall.

When he launched Tarquin's Gin it marked the setting up of the first new gin to be distilled in Cornwall for more than one hundred years.

The small batch operation, which is set in a village near Padstow, makes use of the local spring water and 12 botanicals.

These are...Juniper from Kosovo, coriander seeds from Bulgaria, fresh lemon zest, fresh orange zest, fresh grapefruit zest, orris root from Morocco, angelica root from Poland, liquorice root from Uzbekistan, green cardamom from Guatemala, cinnamon from Madagascar, bitter almonds from Morocco and Devon violets from Tarquin's garden!

Tarquin's Gin is made from a recipe that he crafted over two years. All of the botanicals are carefully selected and steeped in wheat spirit overnight inside the 250 litre copper pot still. In the morning the still is slowly warmed to distilling temperature using a gentle flame.

Over eight hours the first portion of the spirit is discarded, the middle section (or heart) is collected, and the 'tails' from the end of the distillation are also removed.

Tarquin stresses that only the best and most pure spirit makes it into the gin, which is diluted to bottling strength at 42% ABV using local spring water.

To ensure that he creates a distinctive gin, every bottle is filled, labelled, waxed, stamped and signed by hand. Each batch of 300 bottles or less of the award-winning gin has its own character. The description is handwritten on every bottle.

An additional difference is that the still is fired by flame. The myriad of micro reactions in the pot where the copper meets the fire achieves an incredible level of complexity.

Tarquin is not standing still. After creating his gin he has made Cornish Pastis – an anise and liquorice spirit that he reckons is the first UK created pastis!

Telephone: +44 (0) 1841 540121
Email: tarquin@southwesterndistillery.com

Tarquin and his still Tamara.

Tarquin's Gin is distilled in Cornwall.

Tasting Notes

"Nose – Fresh, crisp and vibrant juniper. Light aromatic spice, orange blossom and a hint of cardamom.

Body – Creamy, dry with delicate green pine and subtle frangipane.

Finish – Crisp and clean, with lingering spice notes."

Two Birds

Union Distillers Ltd, E7 Welland Business Park,
Valley Way, Market Harborough,
Leicestershire LE16 7PS.

B ased in the Leicestershire market town of Market Harborough, Two Birds took flight in the Spring of 2013 when electrical engineer Mark Gamble fulfilled his dream of creating a gin.

It was a very hands-on process as Mark had designed and hand-built the copper and brass still, which he named Gerard's No 1.

Obviously this is a small batch business with 100 bottles produced at a time and the local countryside plays its part in the award-winning gin making.

Fresh spring water, drawn from the neighbouring Charnwood Hills is added to the botanicals that are used.

The botanicals include juniper, orris root, coriander, and citrus. The fifth botanical element, however, remains a closely guarded secret of Two Birds who claim that it is this mystery element that gives their gin its unique flavour.

Two Birds Speciality Cocktail Gin.

The bespoke still produces London Dry Gin and the distillery's infusion spirits.

Their speciality Two Birds Cocktail Gin has the same ingredients as their London Dry Gin but it is boosted by an added kick of juniper.

The look of the Two Birds spirits is as important as the quality of the alcohol.

The bottles have been meticulously designed and hand decorated with organic inks.

In addition to their gins, Two Birds also produce an English Vodka and an Absinthe.

Telephone: +44 (0) 1858 414256
Email: sales@twobirdsspirits.co.uk

Gerard's No 1.

Tasting Notes

Two Birds London Dry Gin –
"Nose: Well balanced with good juniper, earthy, lovely pine, vanilla, peppery and fresh lime notes. Taste – "Very classic, soft, clean and easy drinking, low tones of vanilla, superb lingering citrus with classic juniper and spice to finish."

Junipers.

Jonathan Clark in the bar.

Pictures: Alistair Devine.

Ordering a gin at the bar of the City Of London Distillery is not exactly straightforward. Indeed it could easily make you or the bartender feel like they've been hit by a dizzying hang-over headache.

All because of the choice that exists behind the bar where – at the time of writing – there are 265 different gins from which to make your selection!

And those include the gins, bottled tops sealed in red wax, that are made right there on the premises…which are smack in the middle of Sweeney Todd territory – just off Fleet Street, the former haunt of the nation's top newspaper journalists.

"We stock so many gins simply because I thought it would be a nice idea to try and have a variety of many of the gins that are around," explains The City Of London Distillery owner Jonathan Clark.

"We don't have EVERY gin. Not by a long way. But we do have the best variety that I think you can get…going from Jenever, to the classic gins all the way through to the American gins."

The City Of London Distillery – or COLD for short – claims to have brought gin distilling back to the City of London for the first time in almost 200 years.

Its speakeasy style cocktail bar overlooks two copper gin stills, Jennifer and Clarissa, named after TV cooks The Two Fat Ladies.

Apart from the intoxicating aroma of juniper and other botanicals, stored in the gin lab that is located next to the bar, and waiting to be used in the gin-making process, there was a

sense of excitement in the air because COLD mine host Jonathan was keenly anticipating the birth of his latest baby…

…The newest gin to be produced by the company he established in 2012. A larger than life, welcoming character, Jonathan beamed as he indicated the still where what he had named The Square Mile Gin was almost ready to be bottled and labelled.

Now Jonathan is a creator of gin but he didn't go through a specialised training route to reach that level. His learning was done at the university of life as he went from general skivvy at the original bar in Bride Lane to, through buying up a small percentage at a time, owning the joint. "So I've gone from bottle washer to chief bottle washer," says a grinning Jonathan.

His humble beginnings in the trade began back in 1976 and as a consequence of application and hard work, by 1996 he owned the freehold of the building and then for 15 years he rented out the bar that has become COLD.

As Jonathan admits the bar has a chequered history. At various stages it has been known as The City Snooker Club and The Golf Club when it was one of a handful of places that were open throughout the afternoon.

During the period he was renting out the establishment Jonathan concentrated on other business interests but about three years ago he discovered that his bar in the City was threatened with closure.

To his astonishment, he was told that his tenant had been running the premises as what Jonathan now euphemistically terms a 'ladies bar' and the licensing authorities were unimpressed. "They had a pile of complaints and I was in danger of losing the lot and was given 30 days to sort it out."

the Pub with 265 Gins!

The unexpected crisis fired up Jonathan's entrepreneurial skills as he took back full ownership of the bar, and desperately collected his thoughts and decided on a way forward – which he discovered across the Atlantic.

"Everyone had done micro breweries in bars. But I saw on the internet that somebody in New York had created a distillery in a cocktail bar. So I flew out to the Big Apple and fell in love with the idea," says Jonathan.

The next hurdle, of course, was persuading the authorities back in London that his notion of having a gin distillery within the walls of a cocktail bar should be allowed to happen.

"At first they gave me two pages of reasons why it would not be possible," says Jonathan.

However he was determined enough to work through all the red tape and satisfy health and safety conditions, including having the copper stills encased behind bomb-proof glass.

And by December 22, 2012 COLD had started distilling gin!

"Now we are the only distillery in the City of London." says Jonathan. "We make City Of London Gin – that's my gin and tonic gin and just today we have started making The Square Mile Gin, which is my premium gin, ideal for a classic Martini.

"We also make Dorchester Old Tom specially for the Dorchester Hotel."

Currently COLD estimates to be making about 20,000 bottles of gin a year.

"We are small," says Jonathan who talks of us witnessing a Gin Wave. "Gin had not been on the crest of a wave for a long time. There are crests and troughs."

Like many of the small distilleries, COLD offers tours, tastings and the facility for visitors to make, bottle and label their own gin.

In the gin lab at COLD there are a bunch of small pot stills – which Jonathan has cheekily named after the seven dwarves – which allow visitors to design, bottle and drink their very own gin.

"All within two hours. And apart from all that we do the history of gin through the ages and masterclasses," says Jonathan. "Because the clients who come here now want to know when, how and the provenance of the gin. They are really interested in the botanicals, which has never happened before.

"Now they want to touch, feel and smell the ingredients of gin – which is lovely."

City Of London Distillery
22 Bride Lane, London EC4Y 8DT
Telephone: +44 (0) 207 936 3636
Email: cold@cityoflondondistillery.com ◼

In the gin lab at COLD there are a bunch of small pot stills.

Tasting Notes

CITY OF LONDON DRY GIN – A crisp and clean gin, which is juniper led with sweet liquorice, angelica, coriander seeds and a big hit of zesty citrus, from fresh pink grapefruit, orange and lemon.

How to Make Your Own Gin!

Making gin is easy. Making good gin is hard. That is a mantra that will ring true with all the gin masters who have devoted their lives and talents to creating exquisite varieties of the drink.

Now gin lovers can enjoy first hand experience of the wonders and subtleties that can play such a crucial part in the creation of gin.

All over the country distillers are offering tours, tastings and gin-making experiences; which makes for a tantalising must-try for anyone who is fascinated by the drink that is having such a fantastic renaissance.

Naturally no book on gin could possibly be complete without a look-see at a DIY gin. So it was part of my remit to have a go.

Cards on table time means that right now there is a clear and frank confession that I most definitely shaped up as a very unlikely gin master.

Not because of any Calvinistic attitude towards enjoying a tipple. During the course of putting the pages of this book together I've been thrilled to encounter many marvellous gins.

But I had always imagined that making alcohol – well, drinkable alcohol – was something that was destined to remain well beyond my grasp.

Attempts at home-made beer and wine had ended messily and unpalatably.

So I was not exactly filled with confidence when I visited the Edinburgh Gin Distillery, housed in an atmosphere-reeking cellar, just a stone's throw from Princes Street and which is over-looked by the majestic Edinburgh Castle, and girded myself for the nitty gritty of making, bottling and labelling my very own gin, as part of The Gin Making Experience that is offered by Edinburgh Gin.

To be fair, the tricky work had been done in advance by Edinburgh Gin's head distiller, David Wilkinson.

To make a single bottle of gin, a miniature 2-litre still had been put into readiness.

A litre of neutral spirit which had been watered down to 50 per cent, had been poured into the still and then the botanicals – the holy trinity of gin, juniper berries, coriander seeds and angelica root – had been soaked overnight.

To turn this into my own custom-designed gin, I was asked to add a series of further botanicals into this preparation.

An array of botanicals were set out. These included, rose hips, star anise, cinnamon, grains of paradise, fennel, a wide selection of peppercorns, pinks, greens and so on, Szechuan, burdock root and a range of citrus peel, lemon, bitter orange and sweet orange.

It's a sort of lucky dip of gin makings. You select four, or possibly five of these flavours, and these are then added into the liquid that is to be distilled.

Having decided that this gin was to be imbued with a peppery flavour, my choice was a few pinches of grains of paradise, and since the advice was that a gin ought to have at least one citrus, some dried lemon peel and bitter orange, and, finally, the warmth and intensity of Szechuan peppers.

Having been warned that you can overdo the amount of botanicals, that was it. The key flavours were chosen. The still was turned on and brought up to around 80 degrees, at which point the alcohol would begin to boil and evaporate, travelling through the condenser coil so that the hot gin vapour would be condensed into a cold liquid that would be collected for my bottle.

After that it was fingers crossed that the mix was right and a wait of about 90 minutes till the gin is diluted with pure water and then bottled and given a personalised label – in my case it read, John's Gin – and after a day, at least, the gin should be ready to taste.

How did John's Gin work out? Amazingly, it was very tasty indeed and as gloriously peppery as I'd hoped. ■

John Millar with his very own Gin!

Favourite Gin Cocktails

GIN AND TONIC *(Pictured)*

Malaria was a real problem for the soldiers of the Raj when they served in India. When it was found that quinine could be used against the disease British army officers began mixing gin, water, sugar and lime with the quinine to offset the medicine's taste.

When a carbonated quinine tonic was created towards the latter part of the 19th Century the development of Gin and Tonic was a no-brainer.

Now of course the G&T has become one of the most popular drinks.

Indeed there is now an International Gin And Tonic Day, which is celebrated on April 9.

To make…

Prepare a Collins glass with a generous amount of ice. Pour in Gin and then top up with Tonic Water. Garnish with a slice of lemon or lime.

Ingredients
2 oz Gin
Tonic Water
Lemon/lime

PINK GIN *(Pictured)*

A Pink Gin can also be called Gin And Bitters and as well as the obvious ingredient, it contains Angostura.

Angostura was created from a secret recipe in 19th century Venezuela and originally used as a treatment for soldiers in the army of South American hero Simon Bolivar when they suffered stomach complaints.

It is thought that the Royal Navy was the creator of Pink Gin when Gin and Angostura were mixed after it was discovered that the bitters could be used as a treatment for sea sickness.

To make…

Pour the gin and Angostura into a cocktail shaker which contains cubes of ice.

Stir and then strain into a cocktail glass which has been chilled in the fridge.

Ingredients

1½ oz Gin

A few (3 to 4) dashes of Angostura

Ice cubes

DRY MARTINI

The classic gin cocktail. One notion is that it was derived from the Martinez cocktail that was served at the Occidental Hotel in 1860s San Francisco.

Other theories include the claim that it was a cocktail devised in the town of Martinez, California or that the original Dry Martini was dreamed up by a bartender at New York's Knickerbocker Hotel.

To make…

You need gin, dry vermouth, a twist of lemon or olive for garnish, ice, chilled glasses and, of course, a mixing glass.

While the glasses are being chilled in the fridge, add ice to the mixing glass, pour in the gin and dash of vermouth to the glass, and then stir the mixture for about 30 seconds.

Then strain into a martini glass and garnish with the twist of lemon or olives.

If you prefer your Dry Martini shaken and not stirred, simply replace the mixing glass with a cocktail shaker.

Another variation is the Dirty Martini which is very much like a Dry Martini but with the addition of a drop of olive brine.

Ingredients
2½ oz Gin
½ oz Dry Vermouth
Twist of lemon or olives
Ice
Olive brine (for a Dirty Martini)

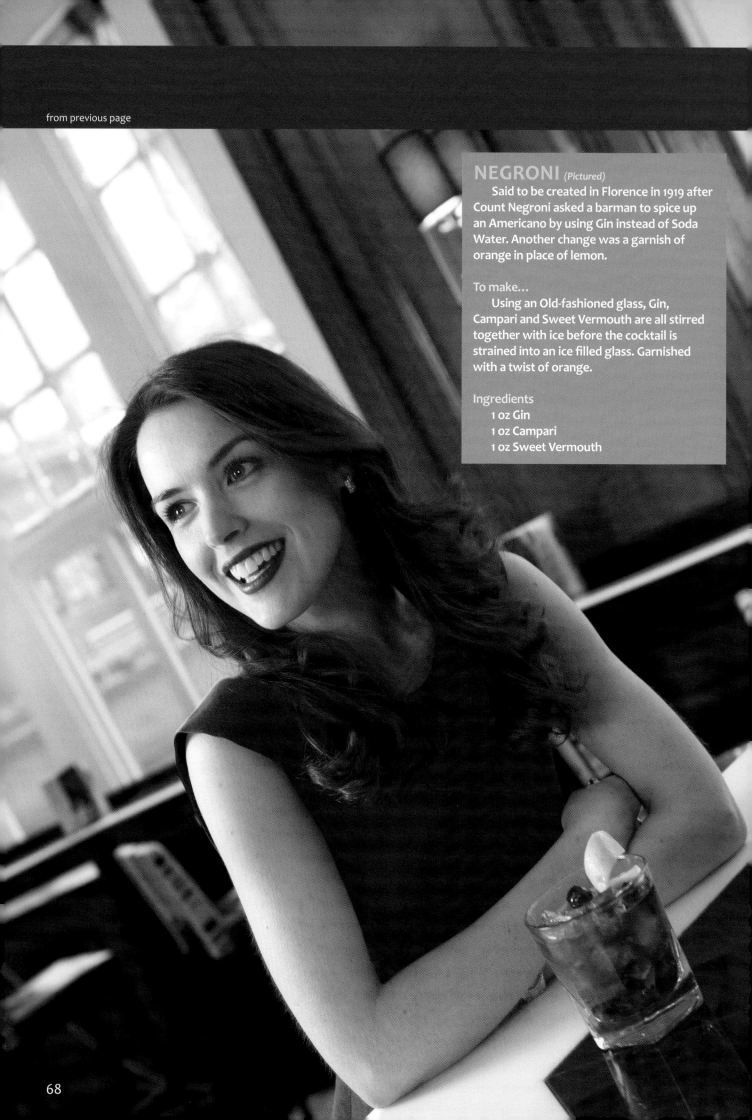

NEGRONI *(Pictured)*

Said to be created in Florence in 1919 after Count Negroni asked a barman to spice up an Americano by using Gin instead of Soda Water. Another change was a garnish of orange in place of lemon.

To make…

Using an Old-fashioned glass, Gin, Campari and Sweet Vermouth are all stirred together with ice before the cocktail is strained into an ice filled glass. Garnished with a twist of orange.

Ingredients
    1 oz Gin
    1 oz Campari
    1 oz Sweet Vermouth

GIN ALEXANDER *(Pictured)*
A few cocktails carry the name Alexander. For instance there is one made with brandy, others use Kahlua or even Benedictine.
This version has a gin base.

To make…
Lemon and sugar is put on the rim of a champagne glass before the gin, white crème de cacao and double cream are all shaken together and then strained into the glass.
The final touch is to sprinkle a little nutmeg over the drink.

Ingredients
2 oz Gin
1 oz white creme de cacao
1 oz double cream
Sugar
Lemon juice
Nutmeg

▶

GIN FIZZ

There are several types of Fizz cocktails. The classic Gin Fizz is served in a Highball glass and possesses a light citrus flavour, since a dash of lime or lemon juice is added to the alcohol.

To make…

The Gin, fruit juice (lime or lemon) and sugar are put into a shaker that's half filled with ice. After lots of shaking the drink is strained into the glass that has been chilling with ice cubes.

Soda Water is then added and a cherry used as garnish.

Ingredients
  2 oz Gin
  Dash of lime or lemon juice
  ½ teaspoonful of fine sugar
  Soda Water
  Cherry

PINK LADY

Another case of take your pick on how this cocktail came about. One theory is that it was invented by American actress and socialite Elsie de Wolfe.

Whatever the source it is a drink that during Prohibition was also known as the Pink Shimmy.

To make…

Pour one white of an egg, half and half cream, Grenadine syrup and Gin into a shaker that has been half filled with crushed ice.

Shake vigorously and then strain into a chilled glass.

Ingredients
  1 White of egg
  1 teaspoon grenadine syrup
  1 teaspoon half-and-half cream
  1½ oz Gin

GIN RICKEY

Back in the early 1880s this drink was originally made with Bourbon and named after American Civil War veteran Colonel Joe Rickey who decided it was to be his tipple of choice.

Then by 1890 it's reckoned that Gin was being used in the creation of the Rickey, which can also be known as the Lime Rickey.

To make…

Gin, lime juice and sugar syrup are put into a cocktail shaker that's been filled with ice.

The mix is shaken furiously before being strained into a glass and then topped up with Soda Water. A slice of lime is used as garnish.

Ingredients
  1½ oz Gin
  Lime juice
  Soda Water
  Sugar Syrup
  Lime slice

Since Frank Sinatra once drank in what is now Champagne Central, the stylish cocktail bar at the Grand Central Hotel in Glasgow Central Station, it seemed the perfect place in which we would have the cocktails prepared and photographed for this section of the *Discover Gin* bookazine. Located in the heart of Glasgow's Style Mile, this opulent bar has stunning original features… from the marble floor, rich furnishings, regal pillars, and of course a marvellous domed ceiling.

SINGAPORE SLING

Originally named the Gin Sling, the Singapore Sling was created early in the 20th century – around 1915 – by Ngiam Tong Boon, a bartender at the legendary Raffles Hotel in Singapore.

There are several variations on the Singapore Sling recipe, some contain Grenadine or Cointreau.

To make…

Gin, lemon juice, simple syrup, and powdered sugar all goes into a cocktail shaker which contains ice cubes.

Shake and then strain into a highball glass with ice cubes.

Pour in soda water.

Use the back of a spoon and pour the cherry brandy over the back of it and into the cocktail.

Garnish with lemon and cherry.

Ingredients
  1½ oz Gin
  1 oz lime juice
  ¼ oz simple syrup
  2 oz soda water
  ½ oz cherry brandy
  Lemon slice
  Maraschino cherry

TOM COLLINS *(Pictured)*

This cocktail has been around since the late 1870s and is traditionally served in a Collins glass.

To make…

The gin, lemon juice and sugar are put into a shaker that has been half filled with ice cubes.

This mixture is shaken and then strained into the Collins glass that contains a decent amount of ice cubes.

The soda water is then added. The drink is stirred and a garnish of cherry and slice of orange is added.

Ingredients

2 oz Gin
1 oz lemon juice
1 tsp superfine sugar
3 oz club soda
1 maraschino cherry
1 slice orange

GIBSON

This is a variation on the Dry Martini and one of the stories surrounding its birth is that it is said to be named after the glamorous Gibson Girl illustrations that were created by the 19th Century artist Charles Dana Gibson.

To make…
Gin and Dry Vermouth are poured into a mixing glass that has been chilling with ice cubes. The mixture is stirred and then strained into a chilled cocktail glass. The classic garnish is two cocktail onions.

Ingredients
2½ oz Gin
½ oz dry vermouth
Cocktail onions

GIMLET

Crime author Raymond Chandler wrote in his classic novel The Long Goodbye that a real gimlet is 'half gin and half Rose's lime juice and nothing else'.

To make…
Pour the Gin and lemon juice into a mixing glass that's had ice added.
The drink is stirred and then strained into a chilled cocktail glass.

Ingredients
2 oz Gin
1¾ oz lime juice

GIN FIXED

A refreshing, sweet and sour flavoured cocktail. Cointreau may be used instead of Triple Sec.

To make…
Put all of the ingredients into an iced shaker and shake before straining into a glass that has been prepared with crushed ice. Stir and serve in a Martini glass with straws.

Ingredients
2 oz Gin
¼ oz Triple Sec
1 oz pineapple juice
½ oz lemon juice
¼ oz sugar syrup

The Champagne Central Cocktail Bar, Grand Central Hotel, Glasgow.
Pictures: Alistair Devine.

GIN & IT

Dating back to the 19th Century, the Gin & It is one of the older Martini cocktails which can also be called the Sweet Vermouth Martini.

The 'It' is an abbreviation of Italian since the sweet Vermouth that's used was Italian Sweet Vermouth.

To make…
Pour the Sweet (Red) Vermouth into a cocktail glass.
Then add the Gin.
Use the Maraschino Cherry as a garnish.

Ingredients
1½ oz Gin
¾ oz Sweet Vermouth
Maraschino Cherry

FRENCH MARTINI

Despite its name this is technically not a Martini because of the absence of Vermouth in the ingredients. Also, this is a drink that can be made with either Gin or Vodka as its base.

To make…
Prepare a cocktail shaker with ice cubes. Pour the Gin, Chambord (raspberry liqueur) and pineapple juice into the shaker.
Shake well and pour into a chilled cocktail glass.

Ingredients
2 oz Dry Gin
¼ oz raspberry liqueur
1 oz pineapple juice

EMERSON

Another classic Martini recipe but one which adds some sweetness to the dryness of Gin.

To make…
Pour the Gin, Sweet Vermouth, Maraschino Liqueur and lemon juice into a cocktail shaker that has been filled with ice.
Shake well and then strain into a chilled cocktail glass.

Ingredients
2 oz Gin
1 oz Sweet Vermouth
½ oz Maraschino Liqueur
½ oz lemon juice

Meet the Number One

Desmond Payne is the world's most experienced Master Gin Distiller. Dublin-born, but with the smooth accent of a classic English gentleman, Desmond has spent a lifetime in the world of gin.

A multiple award winner, and for the last 20 years or so the Master Distiller at Beefeater, you could argue that it was always his destiny that he would be immersed in the business and artistry of gin.

After all, Desmond's mother was from County Cork, the home of another Gin. So, especially if you are a believer in fate, it was always meant to be.

His Irish roots also suggest a sense of adventure, since an ancestor is Tom Park, the first Irishman to cross Africa with H. M. Stanley.

His father served in the Indian Army and another ancestor was a cartoonist, so maybe it is when you put together all of these genetic ingredients that you come up with the special qualities that have made Desmond Payne one of the best in his field.

At the Beefeater headquarters in Kennington, London – in the shadow of the legendary Oval cricket ground – Desmond Payne discussed almost half a century of gin making.

And he revealed how an unhappy gin and tonic that he ordered in the Orient led to the creation of Beefeater 24.

Why did Gin become a magnificent obsession?
DP: It is a long time ago. I have been making gin since 1967. So 47 years ago. I actually started in the wine trade. There was a vague family connection there and I worked in Harrod's for a while when they had a wine cellar and they did a lot of their own bottling. I learned the craft there. I tasted quite a few of them while I was doing the bottling – just to make sure that the right thing was going into the right bottle. Then I left Harrod's to pursue an interest in the wine trade and joined a company called Seager-Evans. There are pictures up there on my office wall of Mr Seager and Mr Evans – they have followed me around for quite a time. They were wine merchants and had cellars below Tower Hill. I worked there for a while. There was an old lift. You had to pull a rope to make it go up or down. They also had a gin distillery in Deptford in East London. It was called Seager's Gin. Now funnily enough I had not seen Seager's Gin for years – the company got absorbed in a series of take-overs – but I am just back from a holiday in Brazil at a place called Bento Goncalves, down in the wine region, and behind the bar where I was visiting there was a bottle of Seager's Gin. It was the only Gin they had. I promptly drank it. Anyway, I joined Seager-Evans as a management trainee. In those days you worked in every department to learn what went on, which is a great way of doing anything. I ended up in the gin distillery and that was it! Why? Because it was so fascinating. There were all these different flavours. My two or three years in the wine trade had helped me develop a sense of taste, I suppose. So there were all these herbs, spices and juniper berries and that was it! The company had a series of management trainees whom they used to send around the world to their other places. For instance there was a Seager's in

Brazil and wineries in Australia, and I got Plymouth! So I worked for Plymouth Gin for a long time. Now Plymouth Gin MUST be made in Plymouth, whereas London Gin – which is what Beefeater is – is a method rather than a location. You can make London Gin anywhere and indeed people do.

It must have been a very exciting time for you as a young man when you embarked on a career in gin?
DP: Yes it was but I think in those days we did not make so much fuss about it. Also we had taken the residual Seager's Gin down to Plymouth, so we were making London Gin there as well. We were then part of Long John Whisky and then Whitbread, and then Allied and so on…

What was the eureka moment, when you discovered that gin was something for which you had a gift?
DP: I don't think that then there was a eureka moment although there was later on when I started developing new products. Then it was just what I did and what I enjoyed doing. So that was great. And Plymouth was quite a change from London in the Sixties. I went from living in a flat in the King's Road, where it was all happening, to suddenly thinking…where on earth is Plymouth? Anyway the master distiller went down to Plymouth when the distilleries were combined there and I went down as a trainee. So that was how I got there.

Was it during your time at Plymouth that you began creating your own gin?
DP: No, that took another forty years. Those were quiet days for gin. Vodka was getting very fashionable, from the late Fifties onwards, so there were some lean times in those early days. It was not a time for new product development. You had the classic brands…Beefeater, Plymouth and Gordon's and Tanqueray. The pubs also had their own label brands, like Squire's Gin and things like that which were jointly owned. But to a certain extent gin had become unfashionable and vodka was sexy and fashionable. But what has happened now is that gin is absolutely back in fashion as are cocktails.

Why has there been this renaissance of gin and the arrival of so many new gin distilleries all over the country?
DP: They are popping up like mushrooms! It is extraordinary and great. There are a couple of reasons. It is partly cyclical, things do go in and out of fashion. The other thing, I think, is that people take much more interest in and pay more attention to flavour. Whether it is in food, drink or whatever. Look at wine. It has changed. When I was a young chap, starting off in the wine trade at Harrod's you only drank wine on occasions. If it was red, it was French and if it was white, it was German. Or it came from the Commonwealth. But you only really had wine on high days and feast days. But what we have seen is a huge explosion. Go to any supermarket and there are yards and yards of shelves of wines. So people are interested in a variety of food and drink, having largely better quality food. And the thing about gin is that it is so versatile. If you look at the whiskies of the world, they all have one thing ▶

Global Gin Master

A portrait of James Burrough, the founder of
Beefeater, hangs opposite Desmond's desk.

Picture: Alistair Devine.

in common – they are all made from grain. Brandy is from grape, rum is from sugar cane. And unless it is flavoured, vodka is a relatively neutral spirit. But when you look at gin, there is a HUGE range of flavours because gin is a flavoured spirit. Now you must put juniper in gin but, beyond that you can add anything you like – as long as it is fresh and decent, honest and legal.

There is a huge range of flavours of gin that people can be much more discriminating about. Not only are there so many styles of gin but gin is also a really mixable drink. I call it a sociable drink, it mixes well.

If you look at the old *Savoy Cocktail Book* of the 1920s then virtually every cocktail there is gin based. Why? Because it is almost a chameleon. In the hands of a good bartender a good gin will go in the direction that the bartender wants to take it. So I am very much aware, as a gin distiller, that what I make here as Beefeater Gin is not what everybody drinks as Beefeater Gin, they drink it as a gin and tonic, or a cocktail or something else. As well as gin being back in fashion, cocktails are back in fashion. So there is that obvious link and our relationship with the great bartenders is very important. They are doing something to the gin before someone gets to drink it. It is the choice of style and flavour, that people can display, that makes gin a fashionable drink. And cocktails are fun!

When did you start going out into the field to research and locate the ingredients for your gin?
DP: It is a matter of being consistent. If you are a brand then you need to be consistent in style, presentation, taste and flavour and everything else. When you are making gin then as I said the only thing that you must put in it is juniper. Now juniper is not cultivated, it grows wild.

The Beefeater Range. For Tasting Notes please see page 4.

Samples of this year's crop of juniper are starting to come in now. We deal mainly through merchants in the UK and most of the juniper we use comes from Italy, from Tuscany. Juniper is a little thorny shrub that I have seen growing in Iceland, in street planters in Chicago, all over the world. The berries ripen about September/October and the juniper berry has quite a thick skin and looks a bit like a blackcurrant but inside it are the oils which give the flavour to the gin. So if you grow juniper in a very cold climate you are not going to develop the oils so much or give as much flavour. So most of our juniper comes from Tuscany and Umbria. It is mostly grown on common land and people get a licence to forage it. They go out and pick juniper berries. I have been out a couple of times to see the harvest and it is hard work. You get two years' crop on the branch at the same time. You get the little, hard, green berries that won't be ripe till the following year and the ripe berries. So you can't cut the branch or you will lose the berries for the following year. What you do is take hold of the end of the branch, with a gloved hand, and knock the branch to shake off the berries. It's rather like collecting olives. Beefeater each year buys in about 50 tonnes of juniper berries. The harvesters in Italy sell on the juniper to a local co-operative or something like that and larger batches are gathered. Then the merchants whom we deal with send in samples and we analyse those samples and decide which we want to buy. We would look at anything up to 200 samples and from that you might only buy three or four. We test by crushing and nosing the berries to decide if it is the kind of thing that we are looking for. Then we get more technical and analytical in our laboratories. We extract the oil of the juniper by distillation and we nose all these oils to see how they come across in distillation. Then we put together a blend that will recreate the Beefeater style that I am looking for, so that it is consistent year on year. That is the most important day in the calendar.

Is it a day you worry about?

DP: It is a day that I do not go out and have a curry and four pints of bitter the night before! (jokes) It is very important because you only get one shot at it. You need to have a fresh palate. And you have to consider that all of the gin trade is doing the same thing, at the same time, with the same people. So you have got to be quick, you have got to be accurate.

Have you ever got it wrong?

DP: Certainly not! Sometimes it is difficult. You can get bad years. But it is critical that you get it right. And some years it is quite easy when there has been a really good crop. But you can never just make do. If you just get one of the elements not quite the same then you throw the whole thing out of balance. It is like making a cocktail. If you put in a little bit too much of sugar syrup or lemon juice then you have suddenly shifted the balance of the drink. The real test of a good bar is you can order a drink three times from three different bartenders and you get the same drink. It is all about being consistent. So being creative and innovative is a different thing and I did not start that until I had forty years under my belt. Not because they didn't trust me – I hope! But with this new generation of gin drinks and great bartenders there was interest. I made Plymouth Gin to the Plymouth Gin recipe for 25 years and God help me if it was different. Then I came to Beefeater – a vastly larger operation – to drive a bigger ship. A portrait of James Burrough, the founder of Beefeater, hangs opposite my desk and if I change his recipe he'll look pretty grumpy. So for years I made Beefeater to the Beefeater recipe.

What about searching out the botanicals? That must be a global event?

DP: Yes and we all do it. But going back to gin. You can make gin just by putting flavoured essences into neutral alcohol and just by giving it a stir. There are plenty of brands made that way. For distilled gin you re-distil neutral alcohol with natural botanicals. With London Gin you can't over-enhance it. But it is being consistent. It's watching the kettle boil. But it has all of this excitement as well, because just before juniper we are looking at coriander seed. Coriander is a cash crop basically. It is extraordinary what happens with coriander. One year everybody will grow coriander. So there is a glut and the price drops. So in Year Two they say they are not going to grow coriander that year, there is no money in it. So there is a scarcity and the price goes right up the top. So in Year Three they all decide there is money in coriander and they'll grow it. So it is a bit of a yo-yo industry. So we would be assessing coriander just before juniper. Coriander again comes from all over the world and it is different. If you get a spice jar of coriander at the supermarket, it is probably Moroccan. I don't use Moroccan coriander in gin because it is a bit more peppery and doesn't give the right balance. So I tend to use coriander from Romania or Bulgaria. Maybe Crimean or Russian coriander. This year has not been an easy year for coriander, not just politically – but that can always affect things. It's that great British thing of taking things from all over the world – like marmalade – and making them very British and then selling them back again.

What is the hardest botanical to come by?

DP: You have to be careful. There are so many new gins and one of the things that makes them different to each other is different botanicals. So people go out and look for rare, interesting and exotic spices. One distiller spent a few months in Africa or up the Amazon, or somewhere, hunting trough the undergrowth for rare botanicals. So there is an element of that. But you have to be careful because if you get too rare and esoteric you are not consistent. I begin to see brands being very regional about their botanicals, which is a lovely idea. But you can be too gimmicky and if you do that then it can be very hard to be consistent.

What was the genesis of you creating Beefeater 24?

DP: We had just changed from being Allied Distillers to being Pernod-Ricard, who have always been keen on innovation and development. Innovation is a very important part of our business. So after 40 years of making gin I was asked to make a new gin, an Ultra Premium Gin. I thought...Yes! At last! My turn! I turned him (the portrait of Mr Burrough) round to face the wall. I'm not entirely joking. And after thinking, at last, Desmond's Gin, I wondered... what am I going to do? Where do I start? Help! I waited for inspiration. But you never know where that is going to come from. Nor do you know – to the chagrin of the marketing department, who have got the labels designed – when it is going to come, either. They gave me a free hand. So when it comes down to it there are only two things that make all these gins different. One obviously is the list of botanicals, where the flavours come from. The other is how you make the gin. And the rest doesn't affect what is inside the bottle. One of the things we do for Beefeater – because James Burrough said so – is that when we charge all our botanicals into the still, to the original recipe, we leave everything in there to steep for 24 hours before we distil, and that really integrates the flavours. They kind of get to know each other before they are all thrown together in a tub of boiling alcohol. It isn't that you get more flavour from that extra time, you get more complexity of flavour and that is a really important thing. So I thought that I was not going to change that 24 hour steeping...hence the name, Beefeater 24. What I needed to look at – for this new gin – was botanicals. The inspiration – the eureka moment – finally, after 40 years, was to use tea! About a year beforehand I had been in Japan – we have a joint venture company with Suntory and I go over there and give talks. They work you quite hard, so by the end of the day I'm ready for my gin and tonic. Beefeater is the No 1 gin in Japan, so that was great. My issue was with the tonic. In Japan you are not allowed to use quinine in foodstuffs, I don't know why, so Japanese tonic water is different. But if the tonic is different then my gin and tonic is different. It is the balance of flavours again. It wasn't what I was used to. But there is more to gin than gin and tonic, so what else could I put in my gin. I looked around to see what soft drinks people were drinking and it was green tea or iced lemon tea and I wondered how that might work in gin. And it is a really good flavour – gin and tea work well together. So I knew that it worked but what I did not know at the time was that the great thing about tea was that the molecular structure of tea means that it fixes extremely well to other flavours. Basically it has got big molecules. I learned this from a great guy called Tony Conigliaro who is a fantastic London mixologist, who deconstructs flavours and understands how they work. So tea and gin worked in Japan, what would happen if I used tea leaf as a botanical in distillation? So I started doing trials, went on a tea tasting course (not as much fun as gin tasting) and distilled different tea leaves to see how they worked with the Beefeater family of botanicals. And you know how it is when you introduce a new member to the family, it may or may not work. There might be fights. Like the son bringing home his girlfriend to meet the family – a scary moment. But she'd better get on with everyone, including grandma' in the corner, or sooner or later there is going to be

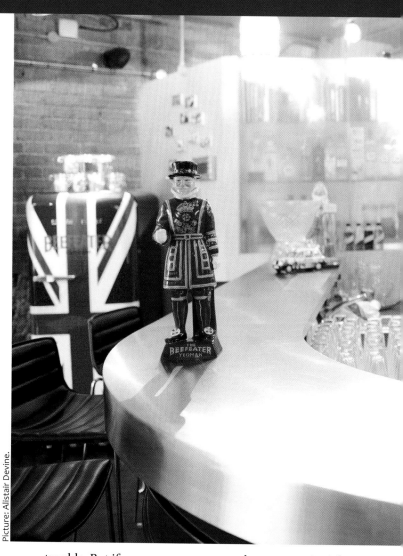

Picture: Alistair Devine.

trouble. But if everyone says great, welcome come in, it has a chance of working but you will still change the relationship with everyone else because there is a new member to relate to. That is what happens with flavours. I tried all sorts of teas, gradually introducing them to all the other botanicals in Beefeater and seeing how they got on. I settled on Chinese green tea and I also used grapefruit. There is already orange and lemon peel in Beefeater and I wanted to introduce a third citrus. One little difference changes the balance so what you have to do is move it on to a different plane but keep it in balance. It is all about integrity, keeping in the things like 24 hour steeping. Otherwise the whole thing collapses and you have lost your credibility.

How long did Beefeater 24 take from inspiration to realisation?

DP: It was 18 months, with the marketing department climbing the walls!

Once I thought I got it, they kindly said it was probably a good idea if someone else tasted the gin. So a tasting panel of the great and the good in the gin industry was put together. There was the prototype of Beefeater 24 against about six other well known brands. We tried each gin on its own, as a gin and tonic, as a Martini with an olive, as a Martini with a twist, as a Collins. The permutation of that was quite a long day. It was

DESMOND PAYNE'S FAVOURITE GIN COCKTAIL – NEGRONI

It is a classic drink. Equal parts Beefeater Gin and Vermouth and Bitters. Pour over ice with a twist of orange peel. That's it. To make it takes about the same time as it takes to drink it. It's easy. I like to keep it simple because the flavours come through.

the fantastic job of going round the world, launching my new gin, State by State through the USA.

You must have a cupboard full of awards?
DP: We (Beefeater) are the most awarded gin.

You must be proud?
DP: I am. But honestly it doesn't really register, particularly. The only moment when I thought...that was me!...was when I was in a smart bar in Athens and on the shelf behind the bar I saw three or four gins that I had developed sitting in a row. I was proud of that. I feel privileged to be doing what I do and I love what I do. Even after 47 years.

In 2015 you'll mark your 20th anniversary at Beefeater, any celebration plans?
DP: No. I've made six gins in the last five years and nothing in the previous 40. I'm not working on anything right now but I would imagine that I will make another gin sometime. The last thing I did was the Burrough's Reserve.

During a social evening out have you ever sent back a drink?
DP: Yes. Sometimes I take a sip and leave it. Sometimes I know they have not served the brand that I ordered. It is very hard to prove. You could argue with the bartender and ruin everybody's evening. But I have sent drinks back...in Kuala Lumpur the cocktail was so badly made that it was wrong.

What are your favourite gin drinks?
DP: It changes. A gin and tonic is a marriage made in heaven. The extraordinary thing is that so much gin lives between finishing work and having dinner as a gin and tonic. A huge amount of gin lives in that little territory. That is why I developed Burrough's Reserve, to say...hang on a minute, it doesn't just have to be then. When I was at Plymouth, one of the great Plymouth drinks was Pink Gin. A dash of Angostura bitters, gin and water...no ice, no nonsense. To me, that is a late morning drink. Of course the gin and tonic is a classic drink, but there are more ways of skinning a cat. Because gin is so versatile in the right hands it will work with so many other flavours. Another favourite is the Negroni, a proper grown-up drink for a start. There is no dilution. There is no tonic water. It is all alcohol. But that is not the reason I like a Negroni. Actually I do not like drinks to be too strong. The flavours of the Negroni just work together. Equal parts gin, sweet vermouth and bitters. It is a wonderful drink. Another classic is the Dry Martini. There is a wonderful bar in San Francisco called Bix Bar which has 'Our Martini Menu'. It is a tiny booklet, about an inch square, which you open up and it says...Gin of your choice, dry vermouth. That's it. But I am a bit wary of Dry Martinis because they are so strong. Watching a Dry Martini being made is theatre. I hate it when you order a cocktail and they go behind the bar and you don't see it being made. I'd probably include also a Collins because it is such a refreshing drink. ■

scary. Just before all these people arrived, I looked at the gin and I was getting absolutely nothing from it. I had been working on it for a year and a half, all these people were coming and it felt as though I had got too close to it. We did the blind tasting and everyone scored it and it came out in the top two, right across the board. Then we did the same exercise in Manhattan and with the same results.

So all of this regarding Beefeater 24 came out of an unhappy gin and tonic in the Orient?
DP: Pretty much. Yes, that is where the inspiration came from. Of course I could have gone to all sorts of flavour houses but things designed by committee are not always the best. One feedback I got was that people loved the gin but they were not getting much tea from it. That was fine, I was not trying g to make a tea gin. But I did go back and found one more tea – a Japanese Sencha tea which has a beautiful aroma to it.

What about the feedback once Beefeater 24 was finished?
DP: I was in Scotland for a big debate on gin versus whisky and of course I lost the debate because we were in Edinburgh. When I came out of the debate they were showing all the awards results and Beefeater 24 had won the trophy for Best Gin. In Year One! That was a wonderful moment. Then I had

A Heady Cocktail of Riots,

Gin has had a fascinating and turbulent history. Initially it was sold as a herbal medicine before being 'sponsored' by a king and then blamed for plunging a nation into social turmoil.

The origins of the drink are generally accepted to be in the Netherlands, although there is an argument that Italy was the first source of gin.

If we go Dutch, however, then it is the 17th century German-born scientist and doctor, Franciscus de la Boe, who was also known as Franciscus Sylvius, who is credited as the father of gin.

While working at Leyden, in the Netherlands on a cure for stomach complaints, de la Boe came up with a mixture of white spirit and juniper berries which he called Genever.

As a medicine this new concoction was sold in pharmacies as a treatment for everything from stomach ailments to gallstones and gout.

It was during this stage of the evolution of gin that the term 'Dutch courage' was first heard.

During the Thirty Years War – which took place in Central Europe from 1618 to 1648 – British troops were said to be taking 'Dutch courage' when they were given doses of gin.

One theory is that the drink was to help cope with the cold weather, another that it helped them feel a bit braver in battle.

Inevitably the serving soldiers brought gin back to these shores and the popularity of the drink began to grow.

The Dutch connection continued by royal approval, after the Glorious Revolution when William of Orange succeed James II.

After coming to the throne in 1689, William III was responsible for statutes that banned imported French brandy, placed levies on German spirits and encouraged the distillation of English spirits.

This allowed the growth of gin making because anyone could now distil gin after publicly posting notice of their intention to do so.

Gin drinking soared. By 1690 it is estimated that Londoners were knocking back half a million gallons of gin!

The reason for such a craze is clear. Gin was cheaper than beer – which was more heavily taxed – and safer than water, which, often or not, was contaminated and the source of disease.

By the 1720s the poor had become swept away by 'gin madness', as it became known. Gin was a cheap way of escaping, albeit briefly, from a life of hunger and slum dwellings.

It was said then that you could be drunk for a penny, dead drunk for tuppence. The statistics suggest that many followed that philosophy since it's estimated by by the end of that decade the average Londoner was drinking 14 gallons of gin a year which meant the city's annual consumption was 11 million gallons!

Drunkenness was a serious problem. Vice chamberlain Lord Hervey spoke of how London 'swarmed with drunken people from morning till night' while the Scottish author Tobias Smollett painted a tragic and disturbing image of poor people passing out in 'dismal caverns' – as he described the drinking dens.

▶ Gin Lane by William Hogarth.

Palaces and Prohibition

Gin League Table

Of all the gin joints in all the world, now where would you imagine most glasses of gin might be served?

Well, it is extremely unlikely that you'd come up with the right answer. Not even remotely.

Because according to a report by the International Wine & Spirit Research, the biggest consumers of gin are to be found in the Philippines. With a population of about **100 million people**, the Philippines is the seventh-most populated country in Asia and the 12th most populated country in the world.

It is the world's largest gin market, accounting for about half of the global sales of the spirit.

On average it is reckoned that a Filipino drinks around 1.4 litres a year, which is the reason why consumption in the islands is far greater than anywhere else in the world.

The Philippines easily top the Gin League Table, with their consumption almost half as much more than that of the USA and streets ahead of Britain which only manages less than a fifth of the Filipino total.

A reason for gin being so hugely popular in the Philippines might be that it is as cheap there as beer. Among the cocktails favoured by Filipinos are the Ginpo, which is a combination of gin and pomelo juice over ice, and a mixture of gin and pineapple juice.

The strangest tipple though has to be the Expired which is a concoction of gin, beer, menthol sweets and ice!

Even if that isn't something which starts the taste buds tingling, there can be no doubt of the part that gin plays in the life of folk in the Philippines.

For instance, even the nation's top basketball team has a connection with the Filipino love for Gin.

Over the years the biggest team in the islands has been variously named after Gilbey's Gin, before becoming known as the Gordon's Gin Boars and, most recently, the Barangay Ginebra Kings – after the top selling gin, Ginebra San Miguel.

Some interesting statistics thrown up by the league table include that the Dutch – who are credited with the origin of gin after all – do not figure in the gin league top ten and that it remains such a popular tipple in India.

COUNTRY	VOLUME
PHILIPPINES	14,140.00
USA	10,075.00
SPAIN	3,596.25
INDIA	3,315.00
UK	2,831.50
CANADA	712.75
GERMANY	535.50
SOUTH AFRICA	518.00
FRANCE	467.50
ITALY	458.50

Units: Case volumes 000s of 9 litre cases (12 x 750 ml bottles)

Copyright: The International Wine & Spirit Research 2014

Something had to be done. Efforts by Parliament to control 'gin madness' had failed and in September 1736 a heavy hand was employed with the Gin Act which introduced a yearly £50 licence – worth around £7,000 today – for the right to sell gin and that fee made selling gin VERY expensive. Duty was also increased from four shillings to £1 per gallon.

Such drastic measures did not go down well with the populace. To say it was an unpopular legislation is an understatement. Even the Prime Minister Sir Robert Walpole thought the Act was a bad idea.

Only two of these new and very pricey licences were taken up. Outcry led to the Gin Riots and the law was openly flouted as an ocean of illegally distilled gin became available. Crude forms of gin, flavoured with turpentine rather than

By 1690 it is estimated that Londoners were knocking back half a million gallons of gin!

juniper, were readily available. It's even said that in some cases the bootleg gin actually contained deadly elements, such as sulphuric acid.

By 1742 the Gin Act was dumped. Nine years later, in 1751, came the Tippling Act which lowered the licence fee and stated that distillers could only sell gin to licensed retailers.

Significantly it was in 1751, the year of the passing of the Tippling Act, that William Hogarth's famous engraving – *Gin Lane*, a hellish vision of a society caught up in a nightmarish gin epidemic – was seen for the first time.

The Hogarth drawing has such power – a vivid and scary image, for instance, is a drunken, mad-eyed mother dropping her child – that it has been acclaimed as 'the most potent anti-drug poster'.

No doubt Hogarth's work was an important factor in support of the legislation.

The changes to the world of gin, that were imposed by the

By 1830 London was booming.

1751 Act of Parliament, were for the good and by 1757 the end of the Gin Craze was in sight.

The next major stage in the evolution of gin came early in the 19th Century. By 1830 London was booming and the places where gin might be drunk had received a revolutionary make-over with the arrival of the Gin Palace.

These ornate establishments, complete with the illumination provided by gas lighting, were a world removed from the old drinking dens. Charles Dickens was a fan, calling them 'perfectly dazzling' and by the middle of the 19th Century there were 5,000 Gin Palaces in London alone.

By the arrival of the 20th Century, gin was about to be at the centre of one of the most notorious eras in the history of the consumption of alcohol as with the Roaring Twenties came America's decision to ban the production, sale and transport of intoxicating liquors. This was the Volstead Act – the name by which the National Prohibition Act was better known – and the law by which the entire United States of America became an officially 'dry' zone.

But while booze was banned, with prohibition taking effect in January 1920 until the ban was lifted at the end of 1933, drinking went undercover, with thousands of speakeasies appearing across the country.

Prohibition also led to the birth of infamous gangsters and bootleggers such as Chicago mob boss Al Capone.

Bootleg alcohol was made in vast quantities during this period which saw the appearance of what became known as bathtub gin.

A crude form of gin was created by combining cheap grain alcohol with water and flavourings. The large bottles that were used were filled from a bath tap, which gave rise to the description 'bathtub gin'.

And since the bootleg gin – crude, un-aged moonshine – had such a terrible taste, this led to the developing of a series of cocktails, which were dreamed up so that the raw taste might be hidden.

Today of course the quality of gin is strictly controlled and enjoyed throughout the world. ∎

Now Bright Spark John

Snowboarding, scuba diving, surfing and skiing are perhaps not the sports that you might associate with someone who spends much of his working day focused on the subtlety of gin making.

But then John McCarthy, head distiller at Adnams in Southwold, Suffolk, doesn't exactly fit what many might consider to be the typical image of a gin master.

His training was in electrical engineering – with control systems a speciality – but John's switch over to the intricate art of distilling has proved a sensational success.

Among the prizes he has gathered since immersing himself in the world of spirits has been the 2013 Gin Trophy at the international Wine And Spirit Competition for Adnams' Copper House Gin.

distillery worked and there were a few hoops to jump through," says John.

Not the least of the tricky issues to be resolved was an ancient law that meant that a brewer couldn't also be a distiller on the same site.

"We think it was to do with the payment of duty because the duty rate on beer and spirits was different," says John.

"We spoke with HMRC who said they couldn't find the law any more but they knew that it existed. But it did not seem to be on the statute books any more."

So Adnams were told to apply for a distilling licence and see what happened.

"It meant that even when we applied for our licence we still didn't know if we would get it or not," explains John.

"To an extent we were flying by the seat of our pants."

The distillery had been designed without Adnams ever

Copper House Distillery.

Picture: Anthony Cullen.

Not bad for someone who joined Adnams in 2001 as an electrical engineering wiz and by 2009 was right at the sharp end as the company, famous for the beers it has brewed since 1872, embarked upon the brave new world of distilling.

"One of the projects I was given was to install a distillery," explains John. "When the distillery project started in 2009 I designed it. I had to come with how a distillery is piped so we had to design the building to fit."

It was an exciting time for John and the company after chairman Jonathan Adnams was inspired by a visit to the USA and came up with the idea of creating a distillery.

"Until 2009 we had never made spirits and never thought we would. So Jonathan Adnams and I needed to know how a

knowing that they would be permitted to make a single bottle of spirits.

"Part of our application had to be a complete set of working drawings, so that all had to be done first. But we got our licence quite quickly. I think the fact that we had been paying duty for 120 years helped," says John.

Then it was down to John McCarthy to prove the faith that Jonathan Adnams obviously had in him. He got to work with some carefully selected botanicals to discover whether he could weave a magical mixture that would result in a top gin.

"I was sent into the lab where we have a small glass still, to come up with a gin recipe," is how John modestly puts it.

And he readily confesses that his gin making was not an instant success. Not by any stretch of the imagination.

▶

John McCarthy.

Picture: Alistair Devine.

"The first few were awful, I have to say. I think that I tried out about 28 gins before I came up with the two that we use today.

"What was wrong with the other batches? Too many botanicals.

"Nowadays visitors come here to Southwold and we will show them how to make gin on a small scale.

"Back then, I was trying to make gin on a small scale and no-one told me how much juniper, coriander or whatever to put in. And to begin with, I was putting far too much in."

The crucial element, as any gin maker will tell you, was the nit picking business of getting a consistent balance of ingredients.

"It was a case of making 28 batches before I found that balance," says John. "The experiments were over three or four months. I would put the botanicals together to steep and then I'd go away and do my normal job and then the next day I'd distil it."

The proof of the pudding, of course, is in the tasting. Initially a tasting panel was assembled of eight individuals who each possessed a wondrous palate but John soon realised that he'd need to take a more direct route to evaluating his two gins.

"To try and please eight people with wonderful palates was impossible. Eventually my boss said to me to just make something that I liked and not to worry about anyone else. In the end that was what I did.

"I wouldn't say that I that I have a great nose. But if I like it, someone else is going to and I've been quite fortunate that quite a lot of other people like what I like.

"It is really good for me to make something that other people enjoy. As an engineer that never really happened.

"Now I only do engineering on desperate occasions. Like the other day when there was a panic."

John McCarthy appears to be someone who is rarely panicked. Which possibly explains his enthusiasm for extreme sports when he takes a break from his work at Adnams.

"I've always enjoyed extreme sports. I go snowboarding now. I tend to fall over a lot. It hurts," says a grinning John.

"I went surfing once upon a time. I still have three surf boards at home, I really should do something about that. I surfed mainly in Cornwall but once went to Bali and surfed there.

"I did try skiing but was never very successful. I went downhill really fast but control was a bit of an issue.

"Another one of my hobbies is diving, but I have not been doing that for a few years."

Although he might have neglected that hobby for a spell, scuba diving is tied into John's gin making!

"We use hibiscus flowers, which I found on a diving holiday in Egypt. When you arrived at the hotel they gave you complimentary hibiscus tea. I had been unaware of it but after tasting I thought it was really nice and decided to try it when I got back here. Now it is a key botanical in our Copper house Gin."

Before this swift and successful transformation in his

JOHN McCARTHY'S FAVOURITE GIN COCKTAIL – CLASSIC MARTINI
"It is a classic martini using first rate gin and I favour using five parts gin to one part vermouth," says John. "it's a cocktail that is stirred, always stirred, and with lots of ice. I don't tend to use a garnish...maybe sometimes just a twist of lemon. It is a nice, simple cocktail."

career, John McCarthy admits that he had not really been a gin lover. His tipple had been beer.

"Working with Adnams I had no choice," he smiles. "Now I can't remember the last time I drank beer."

John agrees that there has been a gin renaissance. "Five years ago there were about three craft gins, now there are about 200 or 300 world-wide. People are keener than they have ever been to try a craft gin."

And how does he see the future? "There are a lot of gin makers starting up in the UK. The number of gin distilleries will even out. It will plateau. But not for a long while."

And he reckons that life at Adnams will proceed along a creative path. "Possibly one day we will have another gin, but at the moment we have so many other products." These include two whiskies, vodka and a lemoncello, that John devised.

His most exotic concoction however is a drink that harks back to the days of French artist Toulouse Lautrec.

"We have two different absinthes, which started after I found an old French distilling manual. Now we do a green and a red absinthe."

And interest in what's brewing at Adnams clearly holds a wide fascination. The company has around 15,000 visitors a year and visiting to the plant only started five years ago. ■

Gin's Travelling Roadshow

When Chrissie Fairclough's hubby began planning a gin distillery in Glenshee in the Scottish Highlands, she decided, naturally enough, to get in on the act. What she has come up with is formally titled Gin Club Scotland.

What it is in practice is the world's first gin roadshow that goes throughout Scotland and beyond – they have been down to the north of England, over to Northern Ireland, and have a London booking – to provide gin tastings.

At these events around 80-100 different gins are provided to illustrate the many and varied subtleties that exist in different types of the drink.

"We go through all the profiles and differences of the gins that are being tasted," explains Chrissie. "It's really all about how the palate works."

The enterprise was launched on World Gin Day in June 2014 and since then Chrissie's Gin Club Scotland has been rushed off its feet.

And hubby's Glenshee produced gin? Production of that is targeted for the summer of 2015 and her husband Simon promises that it will be a gin style built on his frontline knowledge of modern-day gin-drinkers and what appeals about the palate, packaging and pocket.

www.ginclubscotland.com ■

Shaken, Not Stirred

James Bond isn't only the big screen's most famous – and longest serving – secret agent; the spy who is licensed to thrill is also one of the film world's best-known lovers of gin.

So much so that 007's preference for having his Martini 'shaken not stirred' – which Sean Connery first uttered in the 1964 film *Goldfinger* – has become part of common usage, a catch-phrase of which millions are aware.

Another gin related catch-phrase from the silver screen, of course, is featured in the 1942 film classic *Casablanca* when bar boss Rick Blaine (Humphrey Bogart) delivers the timeless line...'of all the gin joints in all the towns in all the world, she walks into mine.'

Back to Bond, the agent's creator, Ian Fleming, made it clear from the outset that his character was going to be very particular about his favourite tipple.

In *Casino Royale*, the Bond book that, in 1953, introduced us to Fleming's hero, he asks for a Dry Martini and the makings of this cocktail are precise.

Bond wishes his drink to be served in a 'deep champagne goblet' with 'three measures of Gordon's one of vodka and half a measure of Kina Lillet' (a French aperitif wine).

The mixture is then to be shaken until it is ice-cold and 007's final touch is that the cocktail ought to be topped with a large, thin slice of lemon peel.

This 007 concoction was named The Vesper, in honour of Vesper Lynd – a woman that Bond falls for in *Casino Royale* and who was portrayed by Eva Green in the 2006 film in which Bond was played by Daniel Craig.

Perhaps because he has a naval background, Bond also enjoys a Pink Gin, as in the 1965 novel *The Man With The Golden Gun* when he orders that cocktail in a Jamaican bar.

Spooks appear to have a fondness for a gin. In John Le Carre's 1974 novel *Tinker, Tailor, Soldier, Spy*, the journalist turned spy Jerry Westerby is discovered by MI6 agent George Smiley to be enjoying a large Pink Gin in a Fleet Street bar.

Sir Alec Guinness, who played Smiley in two acclaimed BBC TV series, had his Pink Gin movie moment in the 1980 film flop, *Raise The Titanic* when he orders the cocktail, stressing not to skimp on the Angostura.

Continuing the fashion for navy men to drink Pink Gin, the cocktail again turns up on screen in *The Cruel Sea* (1953) when the characters played by Jack Hawkins and Donald Sinden share that tipple in a hotel.

Another movie that illustrates the meticulous makings of Pink Gin is *The Grass Is Greener* (1960) in which Hattie Durant, the character played by Jean Simmons, prefers that the Angostura bitters should be burned with a lit match before the gin is added.

Probably because it just looks so cool, the Gibson is another gin cocktail that features in films and television shows.

For instance, a Gibson is what Cary Grant orders in the Alfred Hitchcock thriller, *North By Northwest* (1959) when he is in a restaurant car on a train journey with Eva Marie Saint.

And more recently, in the award-winning TV drama series *Mad Men*, advertising agent boss Roger Sterling – who was played by John Slattery – was very definitely a Gibson guy.

Cool and stylish is what is conjured up by F. Scott Fitzgerald in his classic 1925 novel, *The Great Gatsby*, when Jay Gatsby has drinks at the home of Tom and Daisy Buchanan. When cold drinks are called for, Buchanan serves up Gin Rickey.

In addition to films, television and novels, it is hardly surprising to discover that gin has also been the inspiration for a fair number of songs.

The most recorded number is probably *Gin House*, originally sung by blues legend Bessie Smith and then jazz diva Nina Simone before Sixties pop group Amen Corner – led by Andy Fairweather Low – took it into the pop charts – it reached No 12 – in 1967.

An even more successful pop song is Billy Joel's 1974 hit, *Piano Man* which features the lyric...'there's an old man sitting next to me/making love to his tonic and gin.'

While that line conjures up vivid imagery there is an argument that the wittiest song lyric about gin is contained in a more obscure number.

69 Love Songs – the triple album set from cult American pop group The Magnetic Fields – features a ditty entitled *Love Is Like A Bottle Of Gin*!

On that song Stephin Merritt – singer, songwriter and multi-instrumentalist – intones that...'love is like a bottle of gin, but a bottle of gin is not like love.' ∎